ANOTHER WAY HOME

Moving Beyond Religion to the Interspiritual Jesus and the Sacred Feminine

RUTH ANN LONARDELLI

LUMINARE PRESS

WWW.LUMINAREPRESS.COM

Printed in the United States of America

Cover Design: Claire Flint Last

Luminare Press
438 Charnelton St., Suite 101
Eugene, OR 97401
www.luminarepress.com

LCCN: 2018932790
ISBN: 978-1-944733-57-5

To Nancy

in Memory of Richard Thomas Henry

2-18-49 – 9-10-12

CONTENTS

Don't be satisfied with stories, how things have gone
with others. Unfold your own myth, without complicated
explanation. Everyone will understand the passage,
We have opened you.

Jalalud'din Rumi 1207–1273

PREFACE

One Sunday morning many years ago, when my sister was nine years old, she received a calling as surely as if the angel Gabriel had delivered it himself. It was a typical Sunday, with the exception of a slight disruption at the little Presbyterian Church up the road from where we lived. An out-of-town guest preacher was preaching that day, and the regular Sunday School meeting had been canceled, so everyone, including children, teachers, and all the other adults, could attend the service.

There was a timeless quality to the spring morning, as if the sun was standing still, its rays straining through the deep ambers of the stained glass window, spattering the oak benches with streaks of red and orange. Sunlight streamed into focused shafts of brilliance, scattering dust specks into spinning specks of gold.

Nancy sat in the neatly starched dress our mother had sewn for her: a dress with little flowers, a white Peter Pan collar, and matching white piping on the short-cupped sleeves. She sat on the hard oak bench, fiddling with the church program, trying to work it into a cootie catcher like she had seen our older brother do. It was warm in the tiny church. Two graying gentleman, both in brown suits, opened the ventilator windows. A breeze flowed in, swirling a scent of lilac with the slightest suggestion of road dust.

Lena, the Sunday School teacher, was playing the piano. "A mighty fortress is our God," sang the congregation. "…a bullfrog never failing," sang Nancy with all her heart. She didn't know the word "bulwark," but she knew the word "bullfrog." She loved the spirited song and the way the adults stood as erect as tin soldiers when they sang, their voices loud and forceful, daring yet still safe.

The little church was full of song, light, and spring air. When the last crescendo echoed, Lena reached to steady the canning jar stuffed with lilac blossoms. Without missing a note, she caught the jar midair just before it shimmied off the piano and onto the floor.

Nancy, who was about to slide into her inevitable fidget, came instead to full attention when the visiting preacher began to speak. Soon she was so absorbed that the irregular cootie catcher slipped from her hand and tumbled unnoticed to the floor. The preacher's words exploded like a sneeze gaining momentum, and then softly, like a moist aftershock, lingered for a moment in the air. "Father! Son! Holy Ghost! Jesus on the cross! Lambs and shepherds!" What did he say that transfixed the young girl and set her spinning? She had heard the words before: Jesus on a donkey. Jesus at the well. But this was something more—the preacher, red-faced, pounded a pulse into the old stories until they resonated with her own beating heart.

The preacher paused, licked his lips, dabbed at his forehead with a white handkerchief, and shook his head slowly. His hands were outstretched, uplifted; his eyebrows, arched; his eyes squinted, closed, then wide and rolled back into a peculiar pattern of wordless exclamation. Nancy's

Ruth Ann Lonardelli

mouth hung open, her eyes dry from staring. She stirred reluctantly at an annoying distraction, and quickly casting a glance sideways she saw someone was crying. She heard another cry—loud gasping sobs—and noticed that almost the whole congregation was dabbing their moist eyes and heaving deep, solemn sighs.

After the service, little Nancy ran all the way home from where the Sunday School bus dropped her off, down the dusty driveway and into the farmhouse. "Ran" is not really the right word—she glided, angel-footed, lightly touching the earth just enough to remain upright. Out of breath, cheeks cool from the rush of spring air, she called out for our mother as she burst through the doorway. Our mother, who was making bread, heard Nancy's call.

"How was church?" asked our mother.

"Oh MY! We heard this preacher! It was wonderful, and now I know what I want to be when I grow up! I want to preach and tell people about Jesus so people cry!"

Mother stopped kneading the bread. Overcome by fear for her blasphemous child, she quickly moved from pounding the dough to thumping Nancy's ear. "Don't you ever say that again, girl! That is blasphemy—a terrible sin! There are no women preachers in the Bible. There are no women preachers, period. You are a girl! You can't preach, and you're wicked and full of false pride to think you can. Do you hear me?"

Nancy had never seen her mother so angry.

"Why is it bad? Why can't a girl preach about Jesus?"

Mother twirled her around and swatted her behind. "It just IS; that's all! Never again, do you hear me! I never want to hear you talk this way again!"

Tears filled Nancy's eyes, and the great joy of only minutes ago lay like a chunk of salt in her throat. Now she was breathless from sobbing. She tugged at our mother, who, unresponsive and annoyed, had turned back to her bread dough. Nancy crawled into her secret place far behind the wood cook stove. She didn't know the word "blasphemy." *Blastummy must be something awful,* she thought. Nancy was sure of that much, and she was suddenly afraid. What if her wickedness made God so mad he blasted her tummy wide open? She knew now that she was a wicked girl, rotten and bad, for thinking that one day she could be a preacher.

"I AM SO BAD AND WICKED!" she said over and over again, slipping in and out of a fitful afternoon nap. After this experience, Nancy stuffed her ears against the certainty of her divine calling.

Please understand that our mother was a warm and loving woman. She wanted only the best for us. According to everything she knew from her Primitive Baptist background, the role of women in ministry was clear and unequivocal. Ministry, the expression of Christian ideas and insights, belonged to men. She was sure of this from what she understood of her Christian faith, which she was equally certain was grounded in the teachings of Jesus. She wanted to protect her daughter from spiritual endangerment and douse her troubling spark of enthusiasm in no uncertain terms.

Our mother's strict views were common in those days. Yet they were softer and gentler than the views of our father, who never showed any respect for our mother or his daughters. He openly expressed his disappointment in fathering girls. He was from the old world culture of Italy and steeped in exuberant male dominance. He held a firm grip on his family—my mother and siblings—primarily through an artillery of words. He had a strong talent for verbal and emotional assaults. One glance could stop us in our tracks; his insults and prying interrogations pierced us though. Our father was also a colorful and articulate man. He was a masterful storyteller, and he expected his children and his wife to assume their rightful responsibility as his attentive audience. Listening to the retelling of his stories was tiring. We all knew them by heart. Yet I was fascinated by his method—his passion and presence in the power of story. His stories spilled out through his hands and gestures, his grimaces and laughter. He leaned in at the precise moment to emphasize a word. He knew just when to pause and let the scenes he created catch hold in our imaginations. Even when a barrage of words and images streamed forth from him, he never took his eyes off of us. He scrutinized us, gauging our interest, stopping at times to scold us when our attention drifted. He was a master of timing. He told intricate, multilayered stories of his life as an immigrant laborer. His voice was full of emotion as he spoke of how he had overcome prejudice and poverty to achieve a comfortable life for himself and his family. In my memory, I can hear him putting forth for the umpteenth time the story of his triumph with a field of crops and his endurance over cruel bigotry. My fascination with his techniques must have been similar to what my sister Nancy felt at age nine as she listened to the fiery, itinerant preacher. I felt a sort of awe for the power of words and a pull toward the heartfelt expression of my own deep experiences.

I have also longed to enter into the conversation of life. Like my sister, I inherited the legacy of reticence that was passed on to all the females in our family. I often assumed the role of spectator and listener, playing it safe. I became chronically timid and unable to put forth my own voice in situations that might expose my deepest truth. For years, I managed to silence my call to ministry. Yet I have found other more acceptable and less risky ways to serve through teaching and connecting with people, animals, and nature, until my deepening inner work and spiritual community brought me into the work of ministry.

Nancy grew into an articulate and brilliant woman. She continues to struggle with how to honor her ideas and creativity. She also stridently questions her right to self-expression. She remains spirited, active, and irrepressible, and my most cherished supporter through so many hard times. She continues to explore her life of faith and service, and she has been the kind of committed layperson that makes church possible. Nancy has been instrumental in implementing the caregiving ministry in her community. She has seen befriending others and tending to their needs as the essential human response to our spiritual nature and a meaningful expression of worship.

Together, we watched our mother, oppressed by the tyranny of a culture in which women had no voice, succumb to silence and assume the limited role available to her. We winced at the verbal abuse she received from our father and grieved for the loss of respect she endured. Despite our upbringing and everything we witnessed at home, we grew up in a time when the roles of women were beginning to change.

Although my sister and I have both struggled with diminished self-confidence, we have managed to disallow the depths of oppression our mother experienced.

As times have changed and the opportunities for women in society and in ministry are now so much more open, I

Ruth Ann Lonardelli

have watched with amazement as women have stepped up and spoken out, expressing their own wisdom with power and conviction. Today, I have wonderful women friends in the field of ministry. This is impressive progress. While some churches and spiritual communities are shifting into a more egalitarian phase, the inherent hierarchal nature of such institutions presents challenges. A friend of mine from a progressive church in my area was telling me about their recent ministerial search. When I asked what they were looking for in a minister, she told me they weren't sure, but they had agreed they didn't want a woman. This is not an unusual sentiment. Even in this day, the bias against female ministers endures. Yet integral bonds are still fostered in spiritual community. Revelatory sharing and deep connections of caring are birthed with our hands in the dishwater at church suppers. The platters we serve at those perpetual potlucks are heaped high with love and laughter, and the relationships formed in service and celebration with others hold the promise for authentic partnership communities to emerge and dissolve old patterns of domination.

I often think about my mother's primary objection to women in the ministry. She was certain this went against everything Jesus taught. What she knew, as it turns out, came from men who had interpreted the teachings from their own biases and filters. It is now more commonly recognized that the early Jesus movement was radical with regard to the inclusion of women and much more universal in its teachings than had been thought. Women appear frequently in the stories of Jesus, and the values of the Sacred Feminine feature prominently. Many of the stories are grounded in Greek and Pagan sources, and there are also similarities in the perennial wisdom of other spiritual teachings. Of course, this was before the early Jesus movement congealed into Christianity.

I admit to times of wondering what it would be like if Christianity had never happened. Perhaps there is, as some speculate, a parallel universe. In this world the Emperor Constantine, in 313 CE, made an altogether different decision and withheld support for the Christian faith, a decision that would eventually undermine any possibility of forming the Christian monolith. Perhaps, in this other world, the small communities that formed during the first couple of centuries of the Common Era continued in a vibrant and diverse way, generating new shoots; or perhaps the movement consisting of various beliefs and practices, and inspired by the oral stories of an itinerant Jewish mystic, completely faded from history.

If Christianity had never happened, so much would have been lost. For me, personally, one of the greatest losses would be some of the most beautiful literature, music, and art in the world. It is an inspiring body of work but hardly worth what it cost—that is, the bloody battles, the oppression, and the misery resulting as a consequence of Christianity's reign across the centuries.

Although religious music and art have lifted up my spirits into heights of rapture, and into something I can only describe as sacred and divine, this bliss is tainted by such works as the *Malleus Maleficarium* ("The Hammer of Witches"). This work, devised in the fifteenth century, provided a Christian handbook and rationale for a holocaust that some scholars estimate resulted in the torture and killing of at least nine million women, as well as others considered "a bit odd."[1] Unfortunately, this is only one example of the horror visited upon the planet in the name of Christianity.

Let us say, since we are imagining all this anyhow, that the institution of Christianity never happened. Surely art, music, and poetry are irrepressible and universal expressions of our shared humanity. Something of beauty would have undoubtedly emerged. Let us also speculate that the voices of women, which were commonly heard in some pre-Christian communities, entered into the dialogue of values, spirituality, and the sacred. Where would we be today if the example of Jesus had continued and women were openly invited into conversations of peace, love, and ministry throughout the centuries? What if the inclusion had led to a balanced, partnership model of men and women discovering and expressing their innate divinity and connection to sacred oneness? How would the lives of my mother, sister, myself, and countless other women been different? Unfortunately, we can only imagine.

Just as I was about to shake off the dust, the fallout of all this imagination, and put this first century story of Jesus behind me for good, I felt a tugging at my heartstrings. I recognized who it was right away. It was the same woman who had reached out to touch the hem of Jesus' garment, a woman who was so audacious and determined to boldly stand up for herself that she defied all religious and societal norms to do so. Mary and Elizabeth were also calling me into the conversation as they birthed a new spirituality. It was the woman whose dream compelled her to speak up and object to Jesus' death sentence. It was the ecstatic lover of God who crashed a party as an uninvited guest and without reserve spilled her tears and heart out for the divine.

What am I to do with these women, their teachings and their radical enthusiasm for a new and whole way of being? Am I to leave them there and let their stories exist only as subtext in the larger story of domination and exclusion? I find I cannot leave them behind any more than I can leave my subdued sister and my misinformed mother. I know it is also my own voice straining to be heard, grumbling sometimes within me from the tight space of confinement where I have kept it locked away for decades. It is the unheard voices of so many women of today, of yesterday, and of the future. Perhaps it is time to listen again, just as my mother, my siblings, and I listened again and again to the stories our father told. This time, however, we are listening not for Christianity, but as if Christianity had never happened, and instead we consider stories such as the ones I have chosen in this collection to be possible insights and instructions for women and men. In this age, which is so saturated with intolerance and impelled by global greed and unprecedented technological drivers, and when women of the West are entering a new era of power once exclusively male, there is a desperate need for reconciliation and enduring, deep wisdom. Without this we risk falling into the patterns of violence and hierarchy, those deep ruts in the culture of the West. The good news is we do not have to reinvent everything. There are way-showers in the voices and values of pre-Christian women and in the early Jesus movement, as well as other universal stories prevalent in those times. The following section provides some background into the history and values of the times when these stories were told. You might start there or decide to go directly to the stories in Part Two. Whichever way you choose, hopefully you will find "another way home."

PART I

Old Maps,
New Discoveries

Opening the Door

When I was in my early teens, I had what is called a "born again" experience that changed the course of my life. Soon, I began a personal quest to discover just the "right" church, one that was grounded in literal biblical teachings. I settled into a church and began working in the Sunday School with the younger kids. We often sang a little song together that went something like this: "The B-I-B-L-E! Yes! That's the book for me! I stand alone on the word of God—the B-I-B-L-E!" We would sing this with heartfelt enthusiasm. We marched around as we sang, stomping our feet at the "stand alone" part. This rousing, simple little song was also my deepest truth. I loved the Bible and wanted to learn as much about it as possible. I wanted to know more about how the Bible came to be, the history of the period, and the players involved. In college, opportunities opened up for me to pursue this study further, and I was puzzled when my minister discouraged me from taking any academic classes on religion and the Bible.

Now I understand why my minister was not more encouraging. The more I studied, the more complicated the Bible became for me. The things I thought unquestionably true became open for debate. In church, I learned the Bible to be the inerrant word of God, literal in every sense, and historically accurate. All of this, I discovered, was unfounded. The gospels could not have been firsthand accounts of the life and teachings of Jesus. Early Christians wove their stories together from the thinnest strands of memory. Other elements were added from different traditions that brought in different textures of meaning.[2] A literal interpretation of the Bible was becoming more difficult to defend.

I remember going to my minister with some of my questions. His response was swift and unequivocal: the Bible is to be read literally. To question the literal accuracy of the Bible is the devil's work. The Bible was divinely inspired, and therefore every word must be literally true. There is no room for dialogue. When my minister declared me a lost soul, the church ceased to be a welcoming place for me.

For a long while, I felt like a lost soul. My studies were fascinating and challenging, but my spiritual moorings had slipped loose. I felt resentment toward the churches. I felt betrayed by misinformation and by the lack of support in my quest for truth. I concluded that churches were self-aggrandizing institutions and pathologically intolerant. As a result, I became radically intolerant of them.

However, my search for spiritual understanding did not stop. In fact, I discovered so many fascinating ideas to consider. I studied history, philosophy, psychology, literature, and world religions. I found compassion and a sense of inner peace in Buddhist studies. A new kind of spirituality began to unfold, opening my heart and mind. I am not a Buddhist, but I attribute much of the deepest work I have done to the teachings of Buddhism. The study of mythology, the spiritual stories of world religions, led me to the work of mythologist Joseph Campbell. I began to understand the profound spiritual significance of our religious "myths." Campbell spoke to the purpose and relevance of myth and stories in our lives. Myths, he said, have transcendent properties lifting us into higher awareness.[3] Myths expand our perspective and deepen our understanding of ineffable experiences.

One recurring theme in Campbell's teachings is particularly challenging. He said it is necessary to make peace with the religion of our personal culture and heritage. Making peace with my religious upbringing was not only difficult, it was deeply troubling. Given the misrepresentations of biblical teachings, the abuses of power and authority, and the violence and crimes leveled against humanity, it seemed impossible to make peace with the Christian tradition.

Some years later, I found a way to resolve the dilemma of biblical study. I began to realize there are many ways to approach the texts. One approach is the literal interpretation of the Bible. Another might come from a less literal understanding of the scriptures to a more symbolic, metaphysical meaning. All these viewpoints have validity. There is not just "one way." With these approaches, emphasis is placed on finding value and relevance for authentic, personal, spiritual awareness and development.

When we take Bible stories as having multiple meanings, we harken back to the ancient Jewish tradition of midrash.[4] Stories reveal numerous meanings and unwrap their gifts through contemplation, study, and commentary. Inspired by this idea, I audaciously began approaching biblical understanding by exploring how the stories continue to speak in unexpected ways when seen through a different lens. This became a gateway for me into a renewed appreciation for the tradition of my youth. I began to realize thematic connections I had not seen before. This new approach opened me up to deeper and profound spiritual contemplation.

Some Christian churches do teach this kind of understanding of scripture. Of course, the fundamentalist churches still insist literalism is the only true way. How ironic this is. In the stories attributed to Jesus, he frequently admonished his followers to step outside the material, the literal meaning, and into a deeper understanding.

One amusing example of this is in the book of Matthew (16: 5-12). In this scene, Jesus and the disciples are traveling across a lake for a day of visiting and teaching. The disciples realize they have forgotten to bring along any bread. They begin thinking about the practical matter of lunch. Meanwhile, Jesus is warning them to be alert to the negative influence of the Pharisees and Sadducees. He says, "Be on your guard against the yeast of the Pharisees and Sadducees." The disciples don't understand Jesus' remarks. They turn to each other to discuss what Jesus is saying.

"The yeast of the Pharisees and Sadducees…?" The disciples conclude that he must be referring to the fact that they have forgotten to bring along bread for their meal! They are already beginning to expound on how they will deal with this problem. Perhaps this means they should refuse any bread offered to them. This could lead to proposing a fast or even a new dietary restriction. When Jesus overhears this, he expresses more than a little exasperation at their literal interpretation of his words. "How is it you don't understand that I was not talking to you about bread? But be on your guard against the yeast of the Pharisees and Sadducees." Then they understand he is not telling them to guard against the yeast used in the bread, the material, the literal meaning, but against the subtle and powerful effects of the teachings of the Pharisees and Sadducees. In other words, he is speaking in metaphoric terms. The parables and many teachings of Jesus are presented in just this way—symbolically and metaphysically rather than literally. When we literalize sacred writings, we trivialize their deepest relevance.

From the beginning of the movement, there were countless debates about how to understand the teachings of Jesus. The differences became heated and even violent in the first centuries. Many found meaning in metaphoric interpretations, while others held on to a more literalist viewpoint. Most reputable Biblical scholars agree that even though the early storytellers all had strong beliefs they meant to convey, they understood the stories were not historically accurate. The details of the narratives were not the point. Miracle stories, which are so much a part of the gospels, were common to the culture of those times. Ancient storytellers knew they were borrowing heavily on the cultural influences and the popular stories at the time—stories from Pagan, Greek, and Egyptian sources. Such sources would have been the obvious conveyors of their understandings. In some ways, the thinking of the pre-Christian era was even more insightful than it is today. Biblical scholar John Dominic Crossan observed, "It is not that those ancient people told literal stories and we are now smart enough to take them symbolically, but that they told them symbolically, and we are now dumb enough to take them literally." [5]

The scientific revolution, which began in the sixteenth century, is one of the most influential phases of human achievement. In order for anything to be of value it had to meet the test of empirical, historical evidence. The effect of the new scientific revolution on religion, particularly among religious fundamentalists, was that everything, including matters of faith, had to be verified by hard evidence and facts. In this paradigm, there is little room for the ineffable to work its mystery. In order for any of Jesus' messages to be true, all the details of the stories must also be true. Fundamentalist, literalist, religious beliefs became a response to the emerging worldview. This inevitably limits the value of spiritual storytelling. Music, poetry, art, and stories—all these mediums of the soul—have little, invisible fingers peeling back the layers of reason and touching our deepest sense of self.

Although we don't know whether these stories from the Bible are literally true, there is truth in the stories. Stories are vehicles, or conveyors, of truth; they are not the truth in themselves. In an analogy offered by my friend and teacher, Imam Jamal Rahman, spiritual stories are the vessels that contain a particular substance, but they are not the substance itself.[6] The cup is not the coffee. The cup is just the vessel. The cup is necessary to convey the coffee; but the cup, like the story, is in service to the contents, the essence of what it carries. When we are looking at things from a literal viewpoint, all of our attention goes to the cup. This is my cup! This is my one and true cup! We are focusing our attention on the outer form without looking inside.

The opposite is also true. We can also reject the idea that the stories have any relevance whatsoever. We look at the cup as if to say, "That cup is pink! Porcelain! How silly and sentimental." We push the cup away. Whether we attach ourselves to the cup or reject it, the attention is still on the cup. If we defend or reject the stories with our biases and opinions, we are focusing on the form, the structure, and not on the meaning. Either way we are taking the stories literally. My hope is that someday we can come to approach the gospel stories with curiosity and with more neutrality. When we are offered the cup (the stories), we might say, "I wonder what is inside the cup. I wonder is it sweet? Bitter? Hot? Cold?" We might even venture a sip and taste it, and then decide for ourselves if we like it or not.

Consider the function and purpose of our shared national myths. One story that was told when I was in grade school was of George Washington as a little boy. The story goes that George chopped down his father's prized cherry tree. George's father called the workers and the family together and asked, "Who chopped down my cherry tree?" Following an awkward silence, little George answered, "I confess. I did it."

Many years later in college, I found out there was no fallen tree. No confession. This story is, therefore, not literally true, even though it contains a shared national value. This might not be a realized value, but it has deep meaning for us. We value honesty, integrity, and accountability. We do not expect people to be perfect. We realize we all make mistakes, and we believe, as a nation and as a culture, that accountability is an essential step toward justice and redemption.

Stories are powerful conveyors of meaningful values and messages. They relate essential information and contribute to our understanding in ways that graphs, bullet points, and representations of facts and dates cannot. They open our minds and hearts and stimulate our imagination to help us make wisdom teachings practical. They work best for us when they are not idolized but remain dynamic through thoughtful contemplation. This is especially true of spiritual stories.

What I found in my approach to these stories is so much more meaningful, from a mythic and metaphorical point of view. I began to feel a deep connection with the stories, but also the storytellers who seemed to be speaking from their own experience of transformation. Tom Harpur, former professor and Anglican priest, writes that when we look at the stories in this way, it resolves some of our problems in trying to make sense of the inconsistencies. Instead what is revealed is "…our own potential for Christhood, and for experiencing the indwelling spirit of God here and now, [which] sounds forth in a clear and relevant message for everyone…piercing the literal sense of the Bible to reveal its hidden, allegorical, and mystical inner core…and [offering] new, transformative spiritual vistas and insights."[7]

History is the process of interpreting events by people with particular filters, interests, and biases. When we factor in human error as well, it is impossible to garner an accurate picture of Jesus and his life and mission. We can determine from the Gospels how the authors reflected the thinking of the communities in the pre-Christian era. However, in many ways the gaps in the storylines, the contradictions, and the different points of view raise more questions than they answer, and they obscure a cohesive picture of the historically accurate life and teaching of Jesus.

The Jesus story is about an Aramaic-speaking, Middle Eastern spiritual teacher and mystic. He might have spoken some Greek; however, Aramaic would have been his native language. He would have been known by the name "Yeshua"—the Aramaic form of the Greek "Jesus." He might have read a little. Most likely he did not write anything. The majority of his followers would have been poorly educated, Aramaic-speaking peasantry. For generations, stories about

Ruth Ann Lonardelli

him circulated orally—a tradition relying solely on memory, metaphor, and imagination.

The Aramaic word for God is "Alaha," which translates as Sacred Unity, oneness, wholeness, and completion. This would have been Yeshua's understanding of God. Not a distant, remote, arbitrary entity, but the One Holy Essence, the Sacred within our ordinary lives: Alaha, the Infinite Wholeness in which we live and breathe and that lives and breathes within us. The stories of Yeshua are about a teacher who is also a student. At times, he seems utterly human. We see ourselves in his predicaments. At other times, he appears as the Enlightened One, the Christ, Christ consciousness, an embodiment of both a transcendent spirituality and one committed to the immanent – the sacred in our everyday experiences. Then there are those incidents when he is mysterious, obtuse. Jesus shows up as a catalyst for breakthrough awareness or as a pivotal point in a story. The trajectory of events shifts in unexpected, miraculous ways. All these different perspectives instruct, inspire, and teach us, and, at times, baffle us.

Two broad themes about Jesus are represented in the gospel stories. One theme is Jesus as the great exception, and the other theme is Jesus as the great example of the Christ principle. As the great exception, Jesus alone was God incarnate. He walked among us for a short time, but he was not one of us. He had the mythic qualities of a savior with the powers of a wizard. He was the exception to the human, spiritual experience. This became the dominant tenet of Orthodox traditions, which held that salvation is attainable only through a prescribed belief in a supernatural Jesus—and through the guidance of the clergy. As the great example, Jesus demonstrated the way to the perennial wisdom of God within us, always available, as a divine potential to be realized. We are called then to awaken to this innate capacity and develop an enlightened awareness of the Christ, the Sacred in our own lives. Whether or not Jesus is the notable exception or the great example, for the most part, the gospels have been read with Jesus at center stage. He is in the spotlight of our attention. All eyes are focused on him to see what he will do or say next.

The death of Jesus is thought to be around 30 CE. The earliest book in the New Testament is not a gospel at all, but the letters of Paul, which date about 50 CE. He never knew Jesus, and his writings do not include details of his life. After experiencing a conversion resulting from a vision of Christ, Paul became a champion of early Christian communities. The earliest canonical gospel is the Gospel of Mark. This gospel was probably written after 70 CE. The Gospels of Matthew and Luke contain copied portions of Mark as well as their own versions. These books were written around 80 CE. The Gospel of John was written even later—around 90+ CE. Many other writings are purported to be from these times. They hold their own distinct version of events. One of the best known is the Gospel of Thomas. Some scholars believe this gospel is among the oldest of the gospel records. Thomas contains sayings attributed to Jesus without any record of his miracles or resurrection. None of the gospels were eyewitness accounts, and they were not written by any of the disciples. Whoever wrote the gospels and the other texts of this period would have had considerable education—something unusual and exceptional among the followers of Jesus.

The first four books of the New Testament—the gospels Matthew, Mark, Luke and John—contain writings ascribed to the life and mission of Jesus. Of these four books, Matthew, Mark, and Luke are called the "synoptic" gospels because they are the ones most similar to one another. These gospels are a portion of the twenty-seven canonized books comprising the New Testament. The word "canon" refers to the books the early church fathers thought to be the most acceptable, inspired, and true texts.

Have you ever noticed how many different Christian dominations and churches exist today? Just glance at a web directory, phone book, or newspaper, and you will find listings for dozens of diverse Christian organizations. Rather than a recent phenomenon, widely different interpretations of Christianity have existed from the beginning of the emergent faith. Biblical scholar Bart Ehrman notes that:

> Historians have come to realize that during the first three centuries, the practices and beliefs found among people who called themselves Christian were so varied that the differences between Roman Catholics, Primitive Baptists, and Seventh-Day Adventists pale by comparison. Most of these ancient forms of Christianity are unknown to people in the world today, since they eventually came to be reformed or stamped out.[8]

In addition to all these groups, there were other versions of sacred texts, most of which have been lost. The one commonality the writings share is they were touted as being first-hand accounts of the life of Jesus from the eyewitness reports of his followers. Debates ensued among groups about which texts were right—the absolute, authentic, sacred word. Disagreements often became hostile and vitriolic. Although plagiarism and forgeries were not condoned, they were common methods used in preparing texts and considered standard practice. Defamation of the character of individuals and different groups and slander was widely used in the service of self-promotion.

It was not until the fourth century (367 CE) that Athanasius, Bishop of Alexandria, Egypt, chose twenty-seven manuscripts from among the many available texts. These formed the basis for the New Testament canon. Although it might have appeared there had been consensus all along, and the accepted texts met with approval as being the "right," "inspired," or most "accurate" ones, this is hardly the full story. Bitter feuds and mean-spirited tactics became the standard practice used to suppress and eliminate many of the other writings. The arguments went on for hundreds of years after Athanasius' promotion of the twenty-seven. The different churches of that time period did not unanimously recognize the selection of these chosen books. At the heart of the debates was the wide range of opinions as to the correct interpretation and theology of the Jesus movement. During this time there were many different Christian churches, each one espousing their own point of view and touting their own versions of "authentic" scripture.

Ehrman summarizes the findings of the German Biblical historian Walter Bauer:

> The group that won out did not represent the teachings of Jesus or his apostles. For example, none of the apostles claimed that Jesus was 'fully God and fully man,' or that he was 'begotten not made, of one substance with the Father,' as the fourth-century Nicene Creed maintained. The victorious group called itself orthodox. But it was not the original form of Christianity, and it won its victory only after many hard-fought battles.[9]

We know about some of the lost texts from other writings of those times. Many more gospels were identified and quoted by church fathers, including Clement of Alexandria and Origen, who discredited them. A central "clearing house" of faith developed, which established conformity of ideas. From here, creeds and doctrines originated, forming the common Christian formula and the foundation for the organized Christian church. Even after the texts had been winnowed down to just a few "orthodox" ones, Ehrman notes, "In the ancient world there was no more unanimity about how to interpret a text than there is today."[10] Debates also ensued around when writings should be interpreted literally and when the texts required a more symbolic interpretation.

What survives today as scriptural texts have been copied and recopied by hand over and over again. Many scribes were not trained; they were merely copyists who could not read. Even trained scribes made transcription errors. Punctuation and word spacing were uncommon, and the script ran together in continuous run-on sentences, which made the text difficult to decipher. After a new copy was produced, the older ones were destroyed. No possibility of verifying their "original" accuracy exists. Before the New Testament began to be reproduced mechanically, it had gone through numerous changes made by the scribes, either intentionally or unintentionally. When scholars compare different copied versions of surviving texts, "… we find that no two copies (except the smallest fragments) agree in all their wording."[11]

In the last 200 years, serious biblical research has accelerated, and combined with recent archeological findings, a more precise method of piecing together the past has evolved. Within the last sixty years, since the discovery of the Dead Sea Scrolls, a wealth of new information has been discovered. These discoveries about biblical history and the history of the early Christian movement once belonged to small academic circles and the clergy. Now this material is more widely available to the general population.

If biblical inerrancy is the main focus of a person's religious belief, then all the information refuting this will be seen as an assault on religious faith. If, however, we approach what we know about this material from a more spiritual and less dogmatic position, we find the sayings and stories we have inherited have the potential to stimulate what I believe to be an inherent inner curiosity. Of course, this strikes at the core of the cultural notion that we are not capable of enlightened personal insight—a belief required to maintain a religious hierarchy.

At the heart of the stories of the Jesus movement—and countless narratives from spiritual traditions around the world—there are individuals experiencing an awakening to the presence of the sacred. These are stories catalyzed by relationships, a relational spirituality, that psychologist John Heron describes as "...a spirituality located in the interpersonal heart of the human condition where people co-operate to explore meaning."[12]

A couple of basic standards can help us maintain a steady course and discern what is true and valuable in our spiritual awakening. With time and practice, these standards can assist us in engendering trust in our own individual process. The first is to come from a place of humility. If we succumb to the skewed human propensity that we alone know the truth, or if we think we possess the one and only way, then we have indeed sinned. The word

Ruth Ann Lonardelli

"sin," in the Aramaic words of Jesus, was an archery term that meant to miss the mark.

The second standard is that spirituality must never lead to violence. Any study of a religious work that advocates, motivates, or inspires violence, or is interpreted to suppress and oppress others, stems from a primal survival level of consciousness. Such views are not representative of an enlightened awareness. This also includes the interpersonal violence of projecting onto others what is our own to settle—the kind of propensity attributed to Jesus in the well-known saying, "Why do you look at the speck of sawdust in your brother's eye and pay no attention to the plank in your own eye?" (Matthew 7:3)

Of course, we learn from each other and from inspired teachers, but true wisdom is an inside job, fostered by a supportive, healthy community. The best spiritual traditions recognize that theology and all the endless religious discourses are entry points. Even more revealing is the ineffable mystery, the divine spark waiting to be illumined in us all.

Philosopher Alan Watts identified two kinds of consciousness.[13] First, "spotlight consciousness," which is highly focused and specifically fixates on one thing at a time and does not include peripheral details. The second is "floodlight consciousness," the ability to absorb and integrate information from a broad field of possibilities and subtle messages. According to Watts, as a culture we tend to identify with and specialize in the limited perceptive of spotlight consciousness. We are aware of little beyond what is central in our awareness. In order to understand the spiritual teachings of the Jesus story, we need to shift our perspective from the spotlight on the person of Jesus, his words and deeds alone, to floodlight awareness. This includes a vast web of relationships, events, and meanings. The gospel stories contain a wide variety of characters beckoning us to the edge of our limited vision and pointing toward awakening, *metanoia*: profound spiritual transformation. Some of the attendants of floodlight consciousness lack identifiable form and show up as values, actions, and events. Many of the characters are women.

The Women
Along the Way

One day a friend in my spiritual community turned to me and said, "As a woman, I just don't see myself in the Jesus story." As I listened to her, I thought about the many times I had heard this from others. My friend's words seemed to be bubbling up from a deep well of shared sadness. Her words were also an expression of my own experience.

From what I know about spiritual communities, especially how they are conceived, incubated, and grown into mature, functioning groups, women play a crucial role. At the heart of these movements, they are the ones who show up consistently learning, listening, teaching, and doing the work. If this is true now, women must have been active participants from the beginning. I began to wonder about them and what, if anything, their stories had to teach us. I began to explore the early Jesus movement and, to my surprise, found them—the Marys, Martha, Elizabeth, Suzanna, Joanna, Claudia, Salome, Priscilla, Dorcas, and Phoebe. Thecla, an early convert of Paul, was so popular in her time that she had her own group of devoted followers. Others also showed up: the nameless ones, those archetypal figures who speak for all of us. They are referred to individually as "the woman," "daughter," or collectively as "the women." There are also the more well-known stories of Mary Magdalene, who was revered in early Christian communities and identified as the "best-known disciple of Jesus."[14]

Fragments have been found of a Gospel of Mary Magdala, which exist from the first part of the second century. This narrative presents a different view of Jesus. The text does not preach to the idea of Jesus' ordeal and death as a means to salvation, rather it speaks of Jesus' teachings as a way to inner spiritual awakening. Also, instead of depicting Mary of Magdala as a prostitute, she is seen as a respected, legitimate leader in the early Christian community. Biblical scholar Karen King writes, "It presents the most straightforward and convincing argument in any early Christian writing for the legitimacy of women's leadership; it offers a sharp critique of illegitimate power...and it asks us to rethink the basis for church authority. [15]

In the Bible study classes of my youth, I learned the women in the stories were only present as support for the men and the movement. However, the more I studied and listened, I came to realize how much of such thinking devalued and dismissed the importance of those first century women. I began to think of them in a different way: their individual stories represent deep, sacred insights of profound spiritual and planetary significance.

Many scholars agree the years of the early Jesus movement offered women new opportunities to serve and be seen. They were praised and defended by Jesus and featured prominently in the gospel stories. Contrary to the cultural norms of the time, stories about Jesus feature women engaged in open, public discourse. They held esteemed roles as students and seemed to grasp the Christ message more quickly than the male disciples. They found relative freedom in the teachings of Christ. Even in stories without female characters, the values, metaphors, and symbols are often from the feminine viewpoint. Although some of the post-Jesus letters attributed to Paul contain repressive rules for women, researchers conjecture these were added after Paul's death by more conventional thinkers. These changes were an attempt to mitigate Paul's own more genuine, egalitarian views, and they were likely forged by those opposed to female involvement in church leadership. According to Professor Ehrman, this is not merely opposition, but rather a clear misogynistic message ordering women "to be silent and to 'exercise no authority over a man. If they want to be saved, it will be through 'bearing children.'" In other words, women must remain silent, submissive, and pregnant. This is not exactly a liberated view, and one that has done a world of damage over the years.[16]

Paul relied on women as trusted partners and co-workers, conveyers of key messages and letters to the church. He is credited with the revolutionary pronouncement, "In Christ there is neither male or female...." (Galatians 3:26-28) This view challenges gender dominance. Another significant development in the early Pauline movement was the vow of celibacy practiced by many of the followers. Celibacy is thought to have stemmed from the belief that the end times were forthcoming and having children would not be prudent. Children are about the future, and for these believers, the future was doomed. This meant women were freed from child-bearing and more available to do the work reserved for men: teaching, traveling, preaching, and performing baptisms and other rituals. This must have been a time of considerable excitement for women as they stepped into new roles.

Throughout the course of history, women's movements—societies in which women held positions of respect and even reverence—have sprung up and then been eventually suppressed by patriarchal, domination systems. Riane Eisler, social scientist and author, writes of findings from extensive archeological studies revealing robust societies extending back at least to 6500 BCE. Here, a female deity was a primary focus of worship. These cultures existed for centuries in relative peace and prosperity. In predominantly agricultural communities of Asia Minor, southeastern Europe, Thailand, and Middle America, Eisler states, "We find evidence of the deification of the female—who in her biological character gives birth and nourishment just as the earth does."[17] In ancient societies, such as Minoan Crete, where the Goddess and values of beauty, nurturance, and regeneration were revered, the research indicates thriving cultures without a centralized authority. In a worldview difficult to imagine, societies such as these were not based on hierarchical organizational systems, but displayed a sense of mutuality. These people reflect "...attitudes in which linking rather than ranking appears to have been predominant.... The primacy of the Goddess...does not justify the inference that women have dominated men."[18]

In other works by art historian, Merlin Stone, she cites archeological evidence suggesting, "Neolithic and early historic Goddess-worshiping communities were governed by assemblies probably composed of the elders of the community."[19] These leadership groups are thought to be comprised of elder men *and* women.

With advances in the technology of war and the invasion of aggressive, warring northern nomadic tribes, cultures such as the Minoan were eventually suppressed. A domination system, based on ranking and the restriction of the role of women in society and religion, became the prevailing norm. Over generations, these more egalitarian groups were suppressed by people from other cultures who valued a domination system that glorified violence and suppressed values that were life-giving.[20]

Similarly, following the death of Jesus the first century reemergence of feminine values he so clearly modeled met with strong resistance. As the Jesus movement morphed into Christianity, it became a male-dominated hierarchal system. The early church took form from the established paradigm—the values of the Greeks and prevailing Roman occupiers of the time. These were top-down institutions, domination systems with clear roles and prescribed rules. This is contrary to the radical example we find in the Jesus narratives. In these stories, Jesus is, as Eisler notes, "…freely associating with women, which was itself a form of heresy in his time…. Jesus proclaimed the spiritual equality of all."[21]

We cannot accurately identify what was lost in written material and the oral history of the early Jesus movement. As women became excluded from positions of authority in the new faith, more of their stories disappeared. Along with fragments of the Gospel of Mary, evidence of many other texts in which women played a significant role also exists. The Acts of Thecla and the Gospel of Egyptians record the miracle worker power and teachings of these two women: Thecla and Salome. Researchers think they represent countless other stories about and by women. These stories, Ehrman notes, "…were a significant statement of an important stream of early Christianity. Here were women who refused to participate in the constraints of patriarchal society."[22]

By the third century, with the aid of such renowned misogynistic church fathers as Tertullian, women were proclaimed to be inferior to men and were soundly prohibited to teach or baptize. Tertullian called woman "the gate of hell, the devil's doorway."[23] He viciously targeted and defamed groups in which women assumed roles as priests and prophets and shared in church governance. Unfortunately, Tertullian was not alone in his vehement repudiation of women or groups in which females held respected positions.

Considering the purposeful ousting of women from the movement, it is surprising so much evidence of their impact and relevance still exists in the canonical gospels. I did not realize this until one day I experienced a kind of epiphany about the familiar old stories. I realized the stories had been told by ministers and teachers trained in a particular male bias. I began to listen to the stories differently. Another voice was speaking and revealing meaning I had not suspected. I not only uncovered their lost voices, the voices of a group of forgotten women, but I also heard in their stories timeless spiritual teachings for *all* people. Although the Western religious traditions that followed were rigidly patriarchal, a more feminine spiritual perspective was not entirely suppressed. It remained in the background of religious history waiting to be rediscovered.

In his book, *Sins of the Scriptures,* Bishop John Shelby Spong says the attitudes reflected in the Judeo-Christian movement are indicative of a misogyny originating far back into human history.[24] These attitudes are essentially related to prevailing notions about the female body. Taboos, fears, and disgust around menstruation and childbirth generated rules excluding women from participating in religious practices. Not only were women unclean, they were mysterious, powerful, and threatening. The ability of the female body to bleed without dying was a phenomenon defying explanation. Spong believes the rite of circumcision is an irrational response to menses and that it imitates menstruation. Its purpose is to demonstrate that men can also overcome the threat of gender-related suffering and survive. In some parts of ancient Egypt and other regions, circumcision was practiced at male puberty as a corollary to the onset of menses. The difference is circumcision then became ritualized and made sacred in Judaism, while women were altogether prohibited from serving in the temple. Remnants of this ancient taboo are still evident in many churches in which women are prohibited from ordination. Spong suggests, and I agree, we have not yet moved away from the effects of these ancient "irrational male fears" on our psyches. It is our responsibility to bring these issues into the light of day, and for men and women to honestly face these conscious and unconscious fears arising from an imagined threat that has been the shadow force from which a ancient and hostile patriarchy and a present-day misogyny arises.

The many unconscious aspects of our prejudices and fears compound the difficulty in determining and extracting their deep roots. At its most basic level, misogyny belies our ability to accept life on its own messy terms. Author Andrew Harvey makes the point that:

> The feminine is despised fundamentally because it cuts short and balances our fantasies of transcendence by presenting to us the facts of the body, death, and the shadow—because in the Feminine aspect of the Godhead, darkness is as holy as light, suffering is as

essential as joy, and everything that we described as profane is in fact lit up with electric, mystical meaning.[25]

There is value in acknowledging and honoring the social and spiritual cost of such misogynistic hostility. Our outrage must motivate us to purposeful action and wise choices, rather than dissolve into bitter divisiveness. We do not have the time, nor should we have patience, for more ideologies of preference. If we allow ourselves to slide into the all too alluring trap of animosity, we perpetuate the same old patterns of violence. We do so to the detriment of spiritual integration and at the peril of destroying planetary life. In order to meet the challenges we face—the results of polarized religious beliefs with an emphasis on separation from the sacred, each other, and the life of the planet—we must take a strong and powerful stand for more expanded and inclusive ways of thinking. This includes fostering tolerance and respect for people of all faith traditions. All the children are invited to the table of this banquet. *What is it about including all the children that we don't understand?*

As I began listening to stories from the gospels in which women were present, it was almost as if they were waving to me from the distant past. They were the forgotten ones, waiting at the intersection of history, myth, and tradition for a caravan to stop and bring them along into the story. The emotion this engendered in me was surprising. I felt a sense of deep connection and homecoming. My search became less historical and more like a spiritual family reunion, a profound awakening that was bringing me into a fuller experience of the sacred. I had found my spiritual birth mothers.

Why hadn't I seen it before? Perhaps it was, as poet T.S. Elliot wrote, a matter of "not known because not looked for...."[26] It was all there in plain sight. Women hold the story in place. They are present at the beginning in the miraculous birth, and they are witnesses to the empty tomb at the end. Because of our spotlight filters, set for a patriarchal perspective, we have missed powerful spiritual messages along the way. When we adjust our lens to a wider setting, the stories jump out at us from the shadows into bold relief. What we find is a spirituality that both inspires and uplifts us, and also teaches us how to live. Rather than commandments and taboos, an awakening of our hearts and minds leads us to transformation. This is a much-needed spirituality for our world today.

The teaching of the Sacred Feminine is about a spirituality of deep, meaningful relationship with all of life. In addition to the transcendent, there is also an immanent aspect of the sacred—a teaching central to the Jesus movement. Relationship spirituality is expressed as caring for each other. This is also about a deep respect for ourselves that extends out into how we care for the earth. From this perspective, life and all of creation is sacred expression. This is essential, practical wisdom about how to be in the world and find meaning and value in our everyday lives. The Sacred Feminine is also fiercely protective. When She feels those under her care are in danger, She can be a powerful, protective force.

Language fails us when we attempt to speak of the sacred. We catch intimations in what we call God, Spirit, and Alaha by identifying two main distinctions. These glimpses of the ineffable offer us a fuller experience of our essential oneness. These two ways are the transcendent (father) and the immanent (mother) aspects of God. It is essential to note these are *qualities* and *principles* expressed as gender references, but they are not specifically gendered themselves. In other words, both men and women possess these qualities expressed in unique ways. Think of these two aspects as analogous to the yin-yang principles from the east. The yin and yang principles represent the unified expression of the sacred qualities of feminine and masculine in a complementary symbol of wholeness.

The transcendent is represented as the male/father aspect of the sacred. This is the uplifting, powerful presence of the divine impulse transporting us beyond our earthly human story and connecting us to something larger than our own individual experience. From here we gain a valuable spiritual reference point—a large, grand, sweeping perspective. We might think of it as an eagle imbued with keen vision, soaring and gliding above the earth and watching what is going on below. Its promise is freedom from the confines and struggles of worldly experience into an expanded spiritual perspective and liberation. But if all we know is transcendent spirituality, we can find ourselves missing the embodied spiritual connection with life on Earth. God then is outside, separate from our experience, above us, impersonal.

The immanent is the feminine/mother aspect of the sacred. This is Immanuel—God with us. God is within life itself, present with us in our earthly experience. We find comfort for our sorrows and nurturance of our need. This is demonstrated in qualities of compassion, wisdom, and in acts of caring for one another. Its spiritual reference point is interior. Its work often takes place beneath the surface, where germination happens and roots stretch and grow.

Not a majestic soaring eagle, this is more like the humble killdeer, the master of disguise and mimicry, a bird that hides its young in plain sight. Its natural instinct to protect shows up in extreme displays to distract predators. The mother bird throws enemies off by feigning injury, limping, and leading them away from the vulnerable young. It risks itself as a sacrifice to protect its babies.

In gospel stories about Jesus, the Sacred Feminine re-enters the field of spiritual consciousness, and we behold a more complete and whole experience of the God of Oneness. Images from the tradition of the Sacred Feminine are scattered throughout the gospel stories. Values and meanings associated with the Sacred Feminine reveal a new sensibility and spirituality of balance and connection. The richness of the Jesus movement unfolds in a life-affirming way. Along with the transcendent, powerful, and also impersonal presence of God, there is the personal, immanent aspect of the Goddess. Together, as Oneness, they express a view breathtaking in scope, both timeless and infinite. The potential exists for a radical expansion of the heart extending beyond our tribes of family and faith that embraces all families, all faiths, and all of creation. This is the kind of spirituality that offers hope and healing for a world beset by the madness of separation.

Jesus, as the embodied Christ, revealed the Sacred Feminine, or, as the American mystic and philosopher Charles Fillmore said in one of his talks in 1916:

Jesus Christ became the Holy Mother. He was the mother of us all. We are told the Holy Spirit means comforter, but it is more than that. It apparently means healer. It means an advocate. It means a sympathetic friend. It means everything that we can conceive as the helpful side of God. It is accessible to every one of us, and we get it from within ourselves. We must think about, worship the Holy Mother, talk to the Holy Mother, and enter into the Holy Mother consciousness. We must become, in other words, meek and lowly just like a little child crawling to her mother and getting into her lap and resting on the breast of the mother.[27]

Many of the gospel stories offer meaning that differs from most orthodox interpretation. These are stories of a startling integration of the sacred aspects of female and male, immanent and transcendent principles. One example is the story of the prodigal son. Here, the father's unconditional love and acceptance of his wayward son demonstrates the familiar attribute of a mother's love. Would we still be telling the story, two thousand years later, if the roles were reversed? That is, if the story was about a mother and child relationship? Reconciliations between mothers and wayward children are so commonplace they hardly warrant note. The parable of the prodigal son is remarkable and timeless. It transforms the old paradigm of the reserved human consciousness of the father, the transcendent, with the unconditional love of the mother. In this tale, the father (the transcendent) demonstrates divine qualities of the immanent embodiment of Mother God with us—Immanuel. These two sacred aspects, transcendence and immanence, merge in the father of this story and shatter old patriarchal thinking. This endearing story prevails as a carrier for the message of the wholeness of the Sacred, and how wholeness is experienced. Like the family in this story, the parts of ourselves scattered around lost in feelings of separation have truly come home.

Philosopher Ken Wilber, in his work on Integral Theory, refers to the groundbreaking research of social psychologist Carol Gilligan. Gilligan observed notable gender differences in moral development between males and females and mapped ascending stages of growth for both groups. Wilber notes Gilligan's distinctions:

> Male logic, or a man's voice, tends to be based on terms of autonomy, justice, and rights; whereas women's logic or voice tends to be based on terms of relationship, care, and responsibility. Men tend toward agency; women tend toward communion. Men follow rules; women follow connections. Men look; women touch. Men tend toward individualism, women toward relationship.[28]

Wilber summarizes Gilligan's findings by stating that when both males and females advance into higher levels of moral development, the masculine and feminine aspects within find their balance.

Like many of the stories we will be looking at together, the Sacred Feminine shows up to tip the scales of our awareness toward balance and integration. Why is the Sacred Feminine significant? Author and scholar Barbara Walker states, "The mother figure affects the psyche in a different way from father imagery...."[29] One downside of an external transcendent spirituality is, in its extreme, that it tends to make life on Earth less sacred and it favors an otherworldly view. This can lead to a dangerous dissociation with planetary concerns. Indeed many religious traditions, which rely solely on a transcendent God, have rationalized exploitation of the earth. Yet the promise of the early Jesus movement revealed a strong connection with everyday life. "Lo, I am with you always." (Matthew 28:20) Christ is with us; Immanuel is with us. Every day we are hosts and hostesses to the divine. As we recognize and expand this understanding and realize life is sacred embodiment and interconnected, we lean toward each other and all of life with reverence, with respect, awe and care. This is the Sacred Feminine at work within us and in our world. This is an evolutionary shift in spiritual consciousness much like the biological shift that occurred in the mammalian development of compassion. Cosmologist Brian Swimme says, "This care or compassion begins to show up in organic form when you have a bond developing between a mother and her offspring...and it starts to spread."[30] This is the heart and hope in the message of the Jesus movement. The Great Compassionate Maternal Heart of God realized in all people and for all our relations. Such a shift in spiritual awareness offers the promise that men and women will be able to work together in partnership rather than domination. Perhaps then we can, as Riane Eisler envisions, reclaim an ancient model of mutuality, engaging wholeheartedly in a new, just regard for the essential importance and power of putting care into action.[31]

Until we welcome, embrace, and integrate the Sacred Feminine into our spiritual awareness, we fail to receive the fullness of the Christ and the life-giving message of the Jesus movement. Jesus lies stuck in a cosmic birth canal, not fully born in the world as the embodiment of sacred life. The paradox is that all aspects of the divine point beyond itself and beyond duality. Anyone who claims to have the whole picture is deluded, no matter how seductive such hubris might be. Although we can never truly fathom the Allness of God, when we extend our understanding a fuller expression of Alaha—Sacred Oneness becomes available.

Stories from the gospels contain material from many other sources. This content was borrowed and inserted into the text. Some originate from legends and culture of the times. Symbols and metaphors reflect the lived experience. Goddess icons from Greek and Egyptian influences were prevalent in the early Christian movement. The general assumption might have been that the Hebrews were fiercely opposed to Goddess worship, but this is not born out by extensive archeological findings and research, which has revealed many inscriptions dedicated to "Jehovah and his Asherah" (Shekinah, the beloved Mother-God)."[32] The dove, an ancient, ubiquitous symbol of the goddess, shows up in the baptism of Jesus. The voice we hear in the words, "This is my beloved son," is the voice of the Sacred Feminine.

Symbols provide a multilayered perspective, drawing out the wisdom of both the immanent and the transcendent. In this way, the immanent is uplifted, and we experience the transcendent touching us in a more personal way, culminating in integration, wholeness, and oneness. Symbols, myths, and archetypes are the language of Spirit. These stories have endured not because they support a theological or religious viewpoint, but for the compelling reason that they have the ability to touch something in us in a way that is archetypal and deeply connected with our soul.

The stories I have chosen for this collection will be familiar to anyone brought up in conventional Christian faith. They are also part of our common culture. Whether or not you have ever read the Bible, you are most likely familiar with phrases such as "walking on water" or the "prodigal son." Sometimes what stands in the way of going more deeply into their meanings and possibilities is that they are too familiar. Because we have heard the stories so often and many have trickled down into the content of our culture as fragments and aphorisms, we have no reference to their spiritual significance.

Not all the stories I have chosen feature women or are explicitly about the Sacred Feminine, but all are intended to offer the gift of perspective.

The Gift of Perspective –
The Threshold of Insight

In the tradition of Biblical lore, there are many familiar, sentimental depictions of Jesus welcoming the children. Blond-haired, fair-skinned, well-scrubbed little ones dangle from his knee or gather around him attentively. These iconic pictures are meant to illustrate such passages as, "And he said: 'I tell you the truth, unless you change and become like little children, you will never enter the kingdom of heaven.'" (Matthew 18:3) Heaven, as we will discover in the Jesus stories, is not a reference to a lofty afterlife. Heaven is a higher state of awareness, which Jesus achieves in his spiritual development and demonstrates as infinitely available to all of us in the here and now. While Jesus is speaking of innocence in the preceding passage, there is nothing childish or sentimental in his appeal. He is advocating for an innocence of ideas, an emptying of all our cherished notions, and a breakthrough in the illusion of surface appearances. The mandate is clear: to turn, to shift, and to see from another perspective.

The Buddhists speak of "beginner's mind." The Zen teacher, Suzuki Roshi said, "In the beginner's mind, there are many possibilities; in the expert's mind, there are few."[33] In this Buddhist teaching, and in the stories of Jesus, supreme value is placed on benign curiosity, rather than certainty. Curiosity allows us the childlike freedom to be present in our experiences. Curiosity is one of the most life-affirming of all possible states of mind. Neurobiologists observe that when we have a mindset of openness and inquiry, we produce more of the neurotransmitter dopamine, which enhances our positive mental states. Scientist journalist Lynne McTaggart writes in her book, *The Bond*, "When you are in a state of intense curiosity about something, you see into the space between things. This appears to be the way we're supposed to see, because nature has designed us to feel so good when we do. Seeking brings out our natural tendency to stay awake and see the whole."[34] When we can move beyond our stuck mental states and get free of the tyranny of expertise or the filter of our beliefs, we experience a sense of excitement at new possibilities. We tend to perceive things we have not noticed before.

All innovation in the world of form, and all awakening in the world of spirit, starts from a fundamental change of perspective. From this place of beginner's mind, of childlike unknowing, we are now ready to explore, discover, and recover whatever is available for us. We might find what has always been there, but we were unable to see. This powerful breakthrough awareness occurs in a particularly poignant story of Simon, whose nickname was "Peter." Peter was a devoted follower of Jesus and knew him as teacher, master, and beloved friend.

When the Roman soldiers come to arrest Jesus, Peter cautiously follows the entourage of guards leading Jesus away, being careful not to draw any implicating attention to himself. The guards lead Jesus into the courtyard of the high priest. The door closes behind them. A young girl holds watch at the doorway. She recognizes Peter at once as one of Jesus' followers, and asks, "You are not one of his disciples, are you?" Peter replies, "I am not." (John 18:17) In the Gospel of Mark, the woman moves toward Peter. She leans closely toward him, looking deeply into his eyes, before declaring surely he is one who travels with Jesus. Here, he denies it even more vehemently, "I don't know or understand what you're talking about." Peter begins to curse. "I don't know this man you're talking about." (Mark 14:66–72) Peter is at a doorway. Gates, thresholds, and doors are all symbolic transition points leading into new territory. Doorways are common symbols representing the Sacred Feminine. They are passageways from one experience of life into another, a point at which awareness is compressed and stressed before it expands. This is the threshold where all our fears collide. We are pressed to remember our authentic selves, to claim our true identity, and pass into a place of deeper understanding. This is what happens to Peter when a young woman confronts him and looks into his eyes unflinchingly and questions his childish attempts to escape the truth. It rattles him because she sees deeply into his soul. Peter is unnerved and shaken. He is caught deep in self-forgetting and his feeble attempt to deceive himself and others. "And he [Peter] broke down and wept." (Mark 14:72)

Peter's path of insight, like for many of us, fluctuates with degrees of clarity. On rare occasions, Peter seems to grasp the deep meaning in the teaching. At other times, as in the scene on the mountaintop, Peter's focus is on the material plane. In this story, he is experiencing highly specialized spotlight consciousness, rather than the floodlight consciousness of transformation. In another episode, Peter attempts to prove himself spiritually by duplicating the Jesus miracle of walking on water, but Peter overestimates his spiritual development and sinks. He is the one follower known to resort to violence—a course of action Jesus is quick to repudiate. In many ways, Peter is in all of us, as we grapple with meaning, seek understanding, and journey in the pursuit of deeper spiritual insight. We experience momentary awareness in which we sparkle like brilliant diamonds, only to succumb to utterly inane human proclivities. We become enslaved by our fears and swept away by magical thinking. We become intractable in our old patterns, beliefs, and opinions.

In the dreadful time following the crucifixion, Peter flees to his home near the Sea of Galilee. He is grief-stricken, horrified. He wonders about the others. Where have they gone? Who will be next? What a sight he is, bursting through the doorway of his little cottage. He is breathless and sweating. Trickles of perspiration run down his cheeks; his eyes are wide, reddened, and wet with tears. His family receives him with great concern. "Peter, what has happened?" He is unable to sort out the words lying heavily inside him like stones. He slinks away, retreating into the corner of his home, drawing up his cloak around him. Peter is inconsolable. The family offers him food and water, and attempts to console him, but he turns from them. How can he bear their questions, their tender expressions of concern? The kindness of his loved ones pierces him. He winces at each gesture and retreats even further.

Peter is in the dazed and scattered state of mind accompanying grief. The turmoil of the last few days, the events surrounding the death of Jesus, and the rumors leave him deeply troubled. His thoughts are a tangled net of fears, regrets, and sadness. He is spiraling downward into a dark night of the soul. But after a while, this despondent character rocking in the corner, weeping and mumbling to himself, begins to wear on the rest of the family. Perhaps it is his wife who says, "Peter, why don't you take the boat out and do some fishing? The fresh air might do you good."

Peter waits until nightfall. Under the protection of the darkness, when no one can see him and approach him with a battery of painful questions about where he has been and what is going on, he heads out for his boat anchored at the water's edge.

Peter finds some of the others taking refuge on board: Thomas, Nathaniel, and two other disciples. He rouses them from their sleep and they move wordlessly through their regular routine. The shipboards creak as they move about, creating an eerie echo rippling across the sea. They pull in the anchor and drift off into waters just deep enough to drop their fishing nets. The ship's hull groans slightly in the current; the sounds of water lapping up against the sides of the boat seem raucous in the stillness of the night. Here on his ship at sea, Peter is most at home. If comfort is to be found, it is here. The stars are bright, clear, and distant. From the village, only the occasional sound of a dog's bark and a night owl calling can be heard.

For Peter, it is another sleepless night; his mind is teeming with thoughts about the events leading up to Jesus' death. He plays the scenes over and over again, recalling the fear, his humiliation at being identified as a follower of Jesus, and the shame of his betrayal.

All night the fishermen drift on the waters of Galilee, their nets dangling into the sea, but, as the story goes, "That night they caught nothing." Night passes. The first light appears—the breath of dawn scatters the darkness. This is a time of transition marking a shift in the story. An illumination is in the works. In the filtered light of morning, a few people begin to appear on shore. Most are fishermen and families preparing to take their boats out for the day.

A voice calls out to them from the shore. "Have you caught anything yet?" Peter thinks nothing of it. Certainly someone is just eager to know news of the catch. But even this taxes Peter to the point of despair. He knows if he does not respond that the fisherman will call out again and again. Peter reaches for his voice deep beneath the heaviness of his grief. He does not bother to look away from his seaward gaze, as he calls back, "No, not a thing." How strange his voice sounds to him, its deep resonance belying the tremor in his stomach and his knees. Rather than moving on, the figure onshore remains motionless. Then he calls out simply and clearly, "Friends! Cast your net on the other side!" Peter's reverie is suddenly broken and his breath catches in his throat for a moment. Without hesitation, he moves swiftly. The others move with him, and together they pull the empty nets out of the water, lowering them on the other side of the boat. Right away, the nets are teeming with fish.

The men pull at the nets, struggling to bring in their catch. Fish are jumping into the boat, shimmering in the morning sunlight, tumbling around the decks, slapping the men on their legs, and flipping up onto their chests. The fish begin to pile up, heaps of them cascading out of the net into the boat! "What? What is this?" they wonder. They begin to laugh, and the sound of their laughter echoes out across the water—this laughter is improbable and radical in contrast to the brooding silence of only minutes before.

Ruth Ann Lonardelli

A ripple of recognition circulates among them. First one and then another, until they all discern what has happened. "It is the Christ!" As morning comes and sunlight illuminates the darkness, the divine awareness of Christ dawns on Peter and the others, replacing grief and despair with unimaginable joy!

What has happened here? What lesson did they learn that turns this story around? They had not been told to take the boat off to a different location where their luck would be better. They had not been instructed to use a different method or a better technique. They had been guided to make a shift, a minor movement from one side of the boat to the other. They were led to expand their perspective in order to realize that what they had been looking for was there all the time. What we see in Peter is an expansion of consciousness from being focused, like a spotlight, on what was missing into the floodlight of awareness revealing what was never lost.

Peter's problem, of course, is not only that they were not catching any fish. There was a material need, yes, but the greater urgency was how Peter felt in his heart: his deep loss, confusion, and doubt. Peter was naked, stripped down to pure, raw grief and despair. His revelation is two-fold. What he needs materially is already available. The sea was teeming with fish waiting to be caught. Likewise, Christ was not lost—he cannot be lost—but rather he is timelessly present and available for guidance and inspiration.

Peter's story is what we all experience when we are in a state of grief and worry. In the dark night of the soul, our focus becomes intensely fixed on what seems to be missing. This story is about the spiritual re-truing of ourselves, who we truly are. Peter rides the fluctuating currents of humanness into an expanded awareness. Here is the realization that while we might feel ourselves lost in our grief, the powerfully compelling, sacred guidance of the Christ is always available to us.

This gift of an expanded perspective is the essential opening. The gift leads to the mystic's awareness—the deep experience of connection to our spiritual source, the ground of our being. This shift in awareness is initiated by some insight that might seem quite unremarkable when seen from the outside. Such insight leads us away from the agony of what is missing to the realization of what exists in some most meaningful way. What breaks us open might be as simple as the streak of a cardinal stitching a red thread through the sky as it soars through a perfectly ordinary day, and we are lifted out of our self-absorbed thoughts, our trance of perpetual duties and worries, and we are drawn by this thread as it catches us and carries us to a sense of belonging to all creation. Whatever the catalyst is, we are drawn to a moment of realization moving us from our focus on what is lacking, to what is truly present.

All spiritual transformation begins with curiosity and our response to a vague but persistent sense that there is more going on than we know. The voice of the Christ— divine insight and wisdom—calls us to shift our opinions and our beliefs, and to move a little so we can discover what else is available. We come to understand the meaning of the words attributed to Jesus from the Gospel of Thomas: "The kingdom is spread before us, even though we do not see it."[35]

The mystic follows an inclination to look anew, from spotlight awareness to a floodlight consciousness, and to turn toward the other side for an expanded viewpoint. This is the gift of perspective.

The following stories are much like the call to cast our nets on the other side. It is my hope they will spark, ignite, and burn bright with an expanding awareness to light our way home.

I have included the scriptural text from the New International Version of the New Testament, and then followed the text with my own personal re-telling and commentary. These stories might not be for everyone, and yet they are everyone's stories. It has been my great pleasure to discover how many of them connect with themes and values from other faith traditions. In this way, Jesus cannot be defined and held by any particular faith tradition, but rather his stories and teachings reveal an interspiritual understanding. Within the limited scope of my own knowledge in this area, I have attempted to make these connections explicit whenever they seem apparent to me. These interpretations are the result of personal contemplation; they are not meant to be the definitive or the last word. I am an ordinary seeker who was able to leave behind years of resentment and resistance to the old stories and see them in a fresh and spiritually provocative way. Without intending to be offensive to anyone, I have made them my own through deep reflection. I believe this is as close to their original purpose and intention as we can come. I encourage you to take these stories, spiritual stories from different spiritual traditions, and step right into them, look around, and notice what you see from your own perspective.

PART II

The Stories

Archetypes of the Ordinary: Mary and Elizabeth

In the time of Herod king of Judea there was a priest named Zechariah, who belonged to the priestly division of Abijah; his wife Elizabeth was also a descendant of Aaron. Both of them were righteous in the sight of God, observing all the Lord's commands and decrees blamelessly. But they were childless because Elizabeth was not able to conceive, and they were both very old.

Once when Zechariah's division was on duty and he was serving as priest before God, he was chosen by lot, according to the custom of the priesthood, to go into the temple of the Lord and burn incense. And when the time for the burning of incense came, all the assembled worshipers were praying outside.

Then an angel of the Lord appeared to him, standing at the right side of the altar of incense. When Zechariah saw him, he was startled and was gripped with fear. But the angel said to him: "Do not be afraid, Zechariah; your prayer has been heard. Your wife Elizabeth will bear you a son, and you are to call him John. He will be a joy and delight to you, and many will rejoice because of his birth, for he will be great in the sight of the Lord. He is never to take wine or other fermented drink, and he will be filled with the Holy Spirit even before *he is born. He will bring back many of the people of Israel to the Lord their God. And he will go on before the Lord, in the spirit and power of Elijah, to turn the hearts of the parents to their children and the disobedient to the wisdom of the righteous—to make ready a people prepared for the Lord."*

Zechariah asked the angel, "How can I be sure of this? I am an old man and my wife is well along in years."

The angel said to him, "I am Gabriel. I stand in the presence of God, and I have been sent to speak to you and to tell you this good news. And now you will be silent and not able to speak until the day this happens, because you did not believe my words, which will come true at their appointed time."

Meanwhile, the people were waiting for Zechariah and wondering why he stayed so long in the temple. When he came out, he could not speak to them. They realized he had seen a vision in the temple, for he kept making signs to them but remained unable to speak.

When his time of service was completed, he returned home. After this his wife Elizabeth became pregnant and for five months remained in seclusion. "The Lord has done this for me," she said. "In these days he has shown his favor and taken away my disgrace among the people."

In the sixth month of Elizabeth's pregnancy, God sent the angel Gabriel to Nazareth, a town in Galilee, to a virgin pledged to be married to a man named Joseph, a descendant of David. The virgin's name was Mary. The angel went to her and said, "Greetings, you who are highly favored! The Lord is with you."

Mary was greatly troubled at his words and wondered what kind of greeting this might be. But the angel said to her, "Do not be afraid, Mary; you have found favor with God. You will conceive and give birth to a son, and you are to call him

Jesus. He will be great and will be called the Son of the Most High. The Lord God will give him the throne of his father David, and he will reign over Jacob's descendants forever; his kingdom will never end." "How will this be," Mary asked the angel, "since I am a virgin?" The angel answered, "The Holy Spirit will come on you, and the power of the Most High will overshadow you. So the holy one to be born will be called the Son of God. Even Elizabeth your relative is going to have a child in her old age, and she who was said to be unable to conceive is in her sixth month. For no word from God will ever fail," "I am the Lord's servant," Mary answered. "May your word to me be fulfilled." Then the angel left her.

At that time Mary got ready and hurried to a town in the hill country of Judea, where she entered Zechariah's home and greeted Elizabeth. When Elizabeth heard Mary's greeting, the baby leaped in her womb, and Elizabeth was filled with the Holy Spirit. In a loud voice she exclaimed: "Blessed are you among women, and blessed is the child you will bear! But why am I so favored, that the mother of my Lord should come to me? As soon as the sound of your greeting reached my ears, the baby in my womb leaped for joy. Blessed is she who has believed that the Lord would fulfill his promises to her!"

And Mary said: "My soul glorifies the Lord and my spirit rejoices in God my Savior, for he has been mindful of the humble state of his servant. From now on all generations will call me blessed, for the Mighty One has done great things for me—holy is his name. His mercy extends to those who fear him, from generation to generation. He has performed mighty deeds with his arm; he has scattered those who are proud in their inmost thoughts. He has brought down rulers from their thrones but has lifted up the humble. He has filled the hungry with good things but has sent the rich away empty.

He has helped his servant Israel remembering to be merciful to Abraham and his descendants forever, just as he promised our ancestors."

Mary stayed with Elizabeth for about three months and then returned home. When it was time for Elizabeth to have her baby, she gave birth to a son. Her neighbors and relatives heard that the Lord had shown her great mercy, and they shared her joy. On the eighth day they came to circumcise the child, and they were going to name him after his father Zechariah, but his mother spoke up and said, "No! He is to be called John."

They said to her, "There is no one among your relatives who has that name."

Then they made signs to his father, to find out what he would like to name the child. He asked for a writing tablet, and to everyone's astonishment he wrote, "His name is John," Immediately his mouth was opened and his tongue set free, and he began to speak, praising God.

LUKE 1:5-64 (NIV)

⌖

ELIZABETH AND HER HUSBAND, ZECHARIAH, ARE GET-ting along in years. They are good people, devout and religious. Although they have faithfully followed the temple's rules and laws, something is missing in their lives. The faithful attention of this couple to religious laws, observances, and rituals has not borne fruit. Elizabeth and Zechariah are childless. They are like many of us, who, despite all our best practices and intentions, reach an impasse in our spiritual work, a time when it seems that everything we have done has failed to create the new life we hoped.

One day, while performing the duty of burning incense in the temple, an honor open only to men, Zechariah is visited by the angel Gabriel, who tells him that Elizabeth will have a son and his name is to be John. Zechariah who is startled and incredulous, is not shaken enough that it prevents him from asking *how can he be sure* of this. His request for certainty and proof reflects the rational, analytical mind that is unable to resist the temptation to want to figure everything out. This is monkey mind's chatter about all the obstacles in our way and all the reasons our inspired ideas will not work. This is the part of the mind blocking inspiration and innovation, standing in opposition to the openness of "beginner's mind."

The angel Gabriel clearly recognizes that no amount of explanation will ever satisfy Zechariah. Gabriel has zero tolerance for this need for certainty. With a flicker of his wing, he strikes Zechariah speechless. This part of the mind, the part preoccupied by the incessant questioning about precisely how an idea will be realized, must be silenced in order for sacred mystery to be revealed.

Next the story shifts to Elizabeth. Who is she? She is an older woman at a time of life when women most often become invisible. In her culture, being childless has marginalized her even further. Elizabeth is also a timeless character. Look around and you will find her everywhere. She is a beloved aunt, a neighbor, a friend, the face looking back at you in the mirror. While easily overlooked in a society that idolizes youth, she is a rich field of untapped creativity yet to be realized. Elizabeth's vast life experiences, her solid foundation of faith and even the pain of being different from other women have polished her into a fine jewel of wisdom.

It is not unusual for us to slip into an attitude of cynicism at life's disappointments. Cynicism and resentment deflect the angels of inspiration. Elizabeth meets life with expectancy and openness, rather than succumbing to a mindset of bitterness about missed opportunities and giving in to resignation, which can grind life to a halt. As the embodiment of wisdom, she receives what is germinating within her—the possibility of finally and fully expressing her creative gift to the world. She does so with unquestioning acceptance and profound gratitude. Despite everything she has been led to believe from her culture, it is not too late for her. She accepts this is her time. This is not passive acceptance but spiritual surrender grounded in a mature faith fiercely open to divine possibilities. This openness to mystery, this freedom from cynicism combined with heartfelt gratitude, is the field that incubates the improbable.

Meanwhile, Elizabeth's young cousin, Mary, is also visited by an angel and receives the message that through divine intervention she will be birthing a holy child. I sometimes wonder where Mary was when the angel appeared. What was she doing? Was she inside the modest home she shared with her family? Did the angel loom large in the small space? Did its wings scrape against the masonry walls, casting quivering shadows that spread along the low ceiling? Perhaps it appeared as tiny as a butterfly and flew close to her, lighting on her finger, brushing against her lightly with its delicate wings. She might have been out in the public square, drawing water from the community well. Did she see a curious reflection in the water that unsettled her? Was she walking among the reeds and flowering mustard plants near the river? Did a sudden wind come up rustling the grasses, scattering yellow blossoms? We can only wonder.

But what is clear to us is that the visitation comes to her where she lives, where she walks and rests, where she sleeps and eats. Divine inspiration comes to her in familiar surroundings, close to home. Rather than embarking on some long journey to faraway places in search of the sacred, the sacred finds her. This is a radical shift away from the temple and its limitations to the holy of holies within life itself.

The sight of the divine and the message she receives are fearsome and unsettling. They leave her breathless, trembling, and terrified. How is she to understand it? How does Mary receive the news she will be birthing a new creation? How are we to receive such news ourselves? How does it come to us? Is our fear so strong that when the divine idea does come to us—although we might have prayed and waited for just this moment—rather than listen, we turn away? We know if we heed the call, if we listen and follow the voice of inspiration, much will be asked of us. We will be changed forever.

Mary's response differs from Zechariah's. Rather than asking for certainty, "How can I be sure?" Mary, a virgin, muses about the fulfillment of this prophecy. Her response, "How *will* it be?" affirms the miraculous without doubting the truth of it. The miracle will happen, but how is yet to be revealed. Complex theologies have formed around the anatomy of Mary; however, the original meaning of the word "virgin" is a woman who belongs to no one. This is about autonomy, not anatomy. A virgin, in this sense, is one who follows her inner calling and values, even if she is in relation with another. To be virginal then is a state of inner freedom, clear of prescribed definitions of selfhood imposed by others. Mary is like this. She is aware of all the cultural expectations about her role and behavior, but it is not yet her identity. This inner freedom appears as such a small window in a person's life—but large enough for an angel of possibility to gain entry.

Mary's response to her condition is known as the "Song of Praise." Like Elizabeth's expression of gratitude, Mary's song is also an outpouring of the heart. This song of praise, the Magnificat, is an extraordinary prose poem of celebration and thanksgiving, a peculiar and exceptional response for a young, unmarried girl, who finds herself pregnant. Her condition is extremely dangerous in her culture. She might be stoned to death for being husbandless and expecting a child. Yet the praise she feels and expresses is the kind of thanksgiving that shifts us from an awareness of our problems and their possible consequences into profound gratitude for the mystery itself. Mary is demonstrating one of the most essential lessons of spiritual transformation. Singing a song of gratitude to our problems and concerns is like a mother's lullaby. Our troubles are soothed, and in some miraculous way the breath of our song pierces the density of our worries.

The practice of radical thanksgiving, not necessarily for our challenges, but in spite of them, draws us through our trials with sustaining grace. Mary and Elizabeth share the same ineffable depths of wonder. Wonder is the contrail of the sacred, drawing our attention toward the source. Wonder challenges us to abandon our addiction to the world of mind madness, the perpetual playing of thoughts and our dramas, and to make a clear connection with the sacred.

Mary's role in the Christian tradition has been exalted, praised and deified. All of that has meaning, and we also should not miss the point that Mary was an ordinary young woman. When Mary is made into a symbol of perfection, she is stripped of her humanity and her message. A crucial understanding of this spiritual path is the radical notion that the sacred is embodied within life itself with all its imperfections. In our most ordinary, everyday routine moments, the divine is birthed through us. We become carriers for the sacred, and the miracle is that when we bring this profound understanding into our lives we find Christ everywhere. The seed of the sacred is within every interaction, within nature, and in all of our mundane activities.

Above all, rather than engaging the rational mind and trying to figure everything out, Mary listens for the wisdom of the heart. She demonstrates one of the most powerful spiritual faculties: she knows how to pay attention. It takes humility to listen in this way. Being still, being attentive, is Mary's challenge to us. Discipline and commitment are required to quiet the distractions. Listening opens her. She leans toward the guidance she receives, and radical, sacred love grows within her. She nurtures the divine with her lifeblood. Her body conforms to love's demands. She grows it while it also stretches her.

Like Elizabeth, Mary is free from cynicism, and this allows her to be a dwelling place for the improbable. She is not distracted by the temptations of youth. She wastes no time with frivolous relationships and self-centeredness. She follows her guidance, which leads her to visit Elizabeth the elder, the wise, for companionship as Mary births a new spiritual awareness.

Mary is moving away from the world of doing—the world of commerce, prescribed religious duties, and the machinations of the mental mind—and into the warmth and inner circle of the Sacred Feminine. This sacred company will nurture and foster her growth. Stories in the

Judeo-Christian tradition in which women appear as the central characters, without the presence of men, are rare and of particular significance. Mary, who is at the youthful end of life's continuum, comes unescorted to meet with the wisdom of the older Elizabeth. The two women come together, sharing and supporting each other from their different phases of life experience and in the service of creating a radical spiritual transformation. They combine their powerful, generative gifts of shared values seen from different perspectives. They act as carriers of the sacred through the most primal, natural process of body, blood, and life. They are growing together as key generators of a spirituality with the potential to offer compassion and connection to the world.

Mary arrives at the home of Elizabeth. This is one of the most beautiful scenes in all spiritual literature. She is met with joy and thanksgiving. Elizabeth greets Mary, and Elizabeth's baby leaps in her womb in joyous recognition of the Christ child Mary is carrying. Likewise, when what is being germinated within us is recognized as having value, as being our precious creation, we experience what the mystical Sufi poet, Hafiz, called, "The encouragement of light."[36]

> How did the rose
> ever open its heart
> and give to this world
> all its beauty?
> It felt the encouragement of light
> against its being.
> Otherwise,
> we all remain too frightened.

The encouragement of light is the support, the joyous recognition, we receive from others that nudges us into full bloom, helping us stretch beyond our fears into our most sublime expression of creative potential. This is the powerful and precious gift of true friendship.

Through mutual sharing of experiences and dreams, we reflect back and recognize our truth. Left to ourselves, we might easily brush off what is germinating within us. We reflect back to each other the knowing we are not making this up, something is going on within us. Elizabeth and Mary provide this for each other. Here is the interplay of autonomy and mutual support generating thriving, healthy community. Here is a sacred synergy sparked by sharing our dream in the affirming company of others. "The dance of life," says author, researcher Lynn McTaggart," is not a solo, but a duet."[37]

Unlike the archetypal hero's solitary journey of search and conquest, this way combines an indwelling process, which also allows for relationships. This is about staying still, going within, and timely gestation until the highest and best is brought forth. We experience this in deep communion with each other. When the hero's journey becomes a cult of rugged individuality, we become displaced from our deepest connection with community. This is the hero's shadow side. Strident individuality tends to underestimate the gifts mutuality brings.

In the maternal model, which Mary and Elizabeth represent, we gain an understanding of the interior world in relation to others. This allows for development of our inspired wisdom as well as empathy and compassion, which are powerful tools for transformation. McTaggart reports on findings of integral relationships at the quantum level of existence where "all of life exists in a dynamic relationship of cooperation...a vast web of connection."[38] She describes this dynamic process as "The Bond," a living interconnection most clearly revealing our essential nature, an inherent bias for collaboration and cooperation rather than competition and domination.

The coming together of Mary and Elizabeth, two ordinary women experiencing the universal and natural process of pregnancy and childbirth, reveals the fundamental shift that transforms the old established paradigm. God is not contained only in the temple, an edifice reserved for male priests; God is embodied, right here in our everyday life experiences, as close to us as body and breath. This is Immanuel—God with us, not as a dominating presence, but as an integral, imbued presence of the sacred within our lives. Rather than a hierarchical community, the body of shared experience and relationship emerges. A radical power shift occurs from external to internal, from temple and priest to here, now, and with each other. The inner world and the world of relationships becomes the ground where spiritual transformation germinates, grows, and is realized.

Giving ourselves over wholeheartedly to the sacred, letting it take hold in us, can also be deeply troubling. Our world might feel turned inside out. We are stirred up at our core. Such interior work takes time to incubate. Spiritual life quickens within us and then matures to the point at which it can be expressed. This is a developmental process. Gradual shifts of consciousness accrue in stages and build on each other. This is not about the quick answers, the sound bites. It is a listening work, a waiting work, a maternal season that stretches us and allows the mystery to take place within us.

Labor can be intensely painful. At times, we might need assistance. Sometimes we feel we are past our due date, as if the time of birthing something new will never happen, and our patience and endurance are tested. If we think we will emerge from this process fully realized and spiritually mature, we are mistaken. What is birthed is small, humble, and vulnerable, at first. Joy and exuberance are accompanied by a deep sense of responsibility. We have only just begun.

Elizabeth's time comes and she gives birth to her son. Friends and neighbors gather together for the circumcision ritual and the naming of the child. As the angel had instructed, Elizabeth reports that the child's name is to be "John." According to the cultural pattern, the guests assume the baby will be named after someone in the family. They turn to Zechariah to get his opinion. Zechariah, who is still mute, writes on a tablet: "His name is John!" In this way, he validates Elizabeth, and in doing so, he breaks with the old patriarchal tradition and supports the knowing of the Sacred Feminine. The mystery is now recognized and confirmed by the intellect. The integration of the masculine and feminine ways of knowing has occurred and Zechariah's speech returns. The old authority and paradigm of the law has shifted into a mutually affirming partnership. Love offers the gift of wholeness. When heart and head come together, compassion and wisdom are born.

Twentieth-century mystic Charles Fillmore said, "The conception and birth of Jesus…reveals a soul principle…. That Principle, represented by Mary, is Love. Up to the time of Jesus the feminine principle of the soul, love, never had a chance to express itself because of the arrogant dominance of the intellect."[39]

Stories from the early Jesus movement are not stories of conquest and battle. The acts of Jesus are grounded in compassion and service. Healing, feeding, and being present with other people in relationships—these are all qualities of our Mother-God.

This remarkable story of Mary and Elizabeth is about the emergence of an enlightened heart awareness and connection with the sacred. Meister Eckhart, the Dominican monk of fourteenth century Germany, wrote that regardless of gender we are all called to the creation of this divine realization:

> We are all meant to be mothers of God. What good is it to me if this eternal birth of the divine Son takes place unceasingly but does not take place within myself? And what good is it to me if Mary is full of grace if I am not also full of grace? What good is it to me for the Creator to give birth to his Son if I also do not give birth to him in my time and my culture? This, then, is the fullness of time. When the Son of God is begotten in us.[40]

In this story, the values and lessons of the Sacred Feminine re-enter the consciousness of humankind, bringing what we need to know for our spiritual journey. The Jesus movement—the radical reconfiguration of tradition and the opening of a direct heart path to God—is birthed by ordinary people and the gifts of the feminine aspects of the soul. In this new, emergent paradigm, divine inspiration shows up, not in exotic locations far from home, but right where we are. The chattering objections of the mind need to be stilled so the wisdom of the heart can be heard. Curiosity and openness displace cynicism. A shift occurs from the busyness of the world to the interior world of being. The roles that have been assumed for us and the expectations of society lose their grip. We are neither too old or too young to participate in this new creation. We connect with true companions on this journey; they see our own gifts and also nurture the gifts of others. Mutuality and ecstatic praise become powerful, transformational expressions of grace. We surrender to the sacred by allowing it room within us to grow. The story of Mary and Elizabeth embodies the incremental mystery of spiritual awakening within us. A reconciliation of head and heart leads to partnership rather than domination. What it offers us is just this: a birthing of our spiritual nature into balance, integration, wholeness, and into the fuller expression of Immanuel, the realization of God with us.

REFLECTIONS & QUESTIONS

1. Obedience to old religious formulae and rules, and
    fulfilling religious obligations, does not necessarily
    result in the fulfillment of our spiritual potential.
    *Have you had an experience similar to Zechariah
    and Elizabeth when you felt the religious teachings of
    your tradition were no longer fulfilling your spiritual
    needs? What was this like for you? Was there a specific
    moment when you realized this? Is there a story from
    your experience that represents this moment for you, or
    did it happen gradually over time?*

2. The world of the intellect cannot comprehend
    divine inspiration. Eventually, we have to silence the
    chattering mind and open to the mystery.
    *We have all had an experience of over-thinking. What
    are the drawbacks from over-thinking? What is your
    experience of being still? What is your experience of
    listening?*

3. This is not a matter of searching elsewhere. We are
    not lost and looking for answers. We are already
    found and the answers are within us. We embody
    the sacred in our everyday lives.
    *What does it mean to you that your everyday life
    is an embodiment of the sacred? What can you
    identify, where you are right now, that is spiritually
    revealing?*

4. Rather than measuring our value and importance in
    terms of what we do and finding ways to keep busy,
    being present with our interior world incubates the
    holy.

Do you feel more at home when you are doing or being? Is there an uneasy edge to one more than the other? What are some ways to honor and balance both aspects of doing and being?

5. In sacred mutuality, we offer and receive support and celebrate each other's creativity. The people whom we choose as companions in our growth honor our autonomy while affirming our experience.
What does being honored and affirmed look/feel like to you on the receiving end? What does it look/ feel like on the giving end? Are you willing to be the kind of person who can take joy in the creation of others?

6. When we can practice radical thanksgiving, not necessarily for our challenges, but in spite of them, we are drawn through our trials with sustaining grace. Accessing deep gratitude within us, despite all the unknowns and possible peril, and giving voice to our gratitude leads to joyous expectancy. It is "irrational" in the sense that it seems an unlikely response to what might be going on in the surface events of our lives. Yet, it is immensely powerful and provides energy that fuels the birthing process of a new creation.
Identify at least one thing for which you can express unlikely irrational gratitude.

7. Such shifts in consciousness, while exhilarating, can also be deeply troubling. Things we thought we once knew with certainty are challenged. Old patterns and routines that once offered structure and comfort might seem stifling and rigid.

What has been your experience of navigating through such changes in your life? What has helped and sustained you?

8. This is deep, creative work that accrues incrementally. It stretches us as it grows and matures. This is a developmental process and it takes time. It is a listening work, a waiting work, a maternal season that stretches us.
What stages can you identify in your own spiritual life? Can you identify phases you would consider germinating, gestating, and birthing? Are there also quantum shifts?

9. A sense of wonder challenges us to abandon our addictions to the world of mind madness, the perpetual playing of thoughts and our dramas, to pure connection with the sacred.
What causes you to experience wonder? How do you experience this sensation in your body, mind, and spirit?

10. Whatever we create will require ongoing care. We need to assume full responsibility for our spiritual development and move into new roles as birthers, nurturers, and guides for this new creation.
How will you nurture your emerging spiritual life in an ongoing way?

11. When mind and heart come together, we give birth to a fuller understanding of our spiritual nature.
What possibilities exist for you when your head and heart become integrated? What does this mean to you?

12. Meister Eckhart said, "We are all meant to be mothers of God."

What does it mean to you to be a mother of God?

Grandmother Heart: Anna, the Prophetess

*N*ow there was a man in Jerusalem called Simeon,
who was righteous and devout. He was waiting
for the consolation of Israel, and the Holy Spirit
*was on him. It had been revealed to him by the Holy Spirit
that he would not die before he had seen the Lord's Messiah.
Moved by the Spirit, he went into the temple courts. When
the parents brought in the child Jesus to do for him what the
custom of the Law required, Simeon took him in his arms
and praised God, saying:*

> *"Sovereign Lord, as you have promised,
> you may now dismiss your servant in peace.
> For my eyes have seen your salvation,
> which you have prepared in the sight of all nations:
> a light for revelation to the Gentiles,
> and the glory of your people Israel."*

*The child's father and mother marveled at what was said
about him. Then Simeon blessed them and said to Mary, his
mother: "This child is destined to cause the falling and rising
of many in Israel, and to be a sign that will be spoken against,
so that the thoughts of many hearts will be revealed. And a
sword will pierce your own soul too."*

There was also a prophetess, Anna, the daughter of Pha-
nuel, of the tribe of Asher. She was very old; she had lived with
her husband seven years after her marriage, and then was
a widow until she was eighty-four. She never left the temple
but worshiped night and day, fasting and praying. Coming
up to them at that very moment, she gave thanks to God and
spoke about the child to all who were looking forward to the
redemption of Jerusalem.

LUKE 2:25-38 (NIV)

IN THIS STORY, THE INFANT JESUS IS BROUGHT TO THE
temple where his parents will fulfill the custom of offering
a sacrifice following childbirth. It is a curious welcoming
committee. No choirs, no trumpets or harps, no rosy-
cheeked shepherds or bustling angels, only a couple of
elders—an old man, Simeon, and Anna, an elderly prophetess. The similarities and the differences between Simeon
and Anna are notable. Both recognize the presence of the
sacred from the perspective of their tradition and both offer
thanksgiving. Simeon is described as a devout and righteous
man, a familiar sight at the temple where he regularly visits,
praying for this day.

Simeon takes the baby in his arms and looks into the
infant's eyes. For a moment, it seems as if Jesus sees him.
Then the infant's gaze wanders off to places unseen, to
the blurry edges of form and beyond. Simeon nestles his
scrawny, gray beard against the baby's chest and gently
rocks him. This is a poignant and touching scene in which
he recognizes that the child he is holding is the fulfillment

of his own spiritual yearning. Simeon voices a passionate litany of praise. But the gentle, sweet moment passes quickly. Drawing from the religious prophesies of the past, Simeon's declaration of effusive praise turns into a prophetic vision of calamity and disaster. He then turns to the new mother with powerful, troubling predictions about the life of the child, the pain he will cause and the suffering she will undergo. This moment of exquisite connection with the divine is cut short by the intrusion of his old religious views. Simeon's grip on his ideology shifts the peace and bliss of this precious encounter into disquieting prophecy.

Mythologist Joseph Campbell warns about the perils of holding on to old ideologies at the expense of a deeper experience. "You hold on to your own ideology, your own little manner of thinking, and when a larger experience of God approaches, an experience greater than you are prepared to receive, you take flight from it by clinging to the image in your mind. This is known as preserving your faith."[41] For Simeon, his love affair with the newborn Christ, his joy and jubilation, seeks an explanation. Ultimately, he sees the experience through the lens of tradition and religious prophesy. He turns to the mother, Mary, and says what no parent wants to hear. This child will be the cause of much "falling and rising…and a sword will pierce your own soul too."

Anna holds the title of prophetess. Rather than a place she occasionally visits, the temple is her life. She is also steeped in her tradition, which serves as a foundation for her faith rather than a platform. Unlike the wordier and robust Simeon, Anna's response to the baby Jesus is more serene and succinct. "Coming up to them at that very moment, she gave thanks to God." Anna receives the child and parents with straightforward open-heartedness and thanksgiving. She is present to the moment and demonstrates the spirit of the ineffable, which is inexpressible and too sacred, too large to be uttered. This is a deep soul encounter for Anna such as Lebanese poet Kahlil Gibran captures in his poem *Song of the Soul*: "In the depths of my soul there is a wordless song—a song that lives as a seed in my heart."[42] When Anna speaks, she talks about a seed taking hold and a hopeful harvest, a future of spiritual possibilities.

Anna is caught in history, timelessly cast as someone whose years of teaching and practice have brought her to this moment. Anna's greeting is palpably expressive of what happens when deep gratitude, profound love and awe meet the limitations of language: she gives thanks and marvels at the possibilities.

Who is Anna and what is she doing in this story? The author of Luke makes specific note: The old woman is "…a prophetess Anna, the daughter of Phanuel, of the tribe of Asher." For today's readers, these attributions would not be relevant. For people living at the time, this information placed her as a member of a respected family, originating from a different region than most of the locals. All of these factors provided depth to this story for the first century audience. As a prophetess, Anna was honored as a inspirational figure. Finding her sanctuary and sustenance in the temple reveals not only her devotion but also the respected place she held in her community: "She was very old… a widow until she was eighty-four. She never left the temple but worshiped night and day fasting and praying."

Luke was written many years after such an incident took place. This scene cannot be assumed to be historically accurate, although it is generally thought Anna was an actual historical character. At the time of the writing of Luke, she might have existed in the collective memory as a beloved teacher, aunt, or grandmother. Perhaps her place in history went something like this: scribes piecing together the story of the infant Jesus from local legends and hearsay, as well as other written texts, could have been reminded of stories circulating about Anna. Perhaps they thought about how much Anna would have loved to be present with the baby Jesus. This little story fragment then is a tribute to her. Her inclusion is a loving recognition of someone who made a difference in the lives of others and who embodied worship and devotion. She is like the faded image in an old photograph, creased and indistinct, yet her presence in the snapshot at all is evocative. Her presence in this story indicates she was a respected woman in her community. It also tells us something about the status of women. A precedent existed for women to be teachers and prophets. They are in the story as valued participants at the beginning of the Jesus story. We are to give Anna and other women wisdom teachers their place in history. In doing this, we not only honor the contributions of others, we recognize those who tether us, anchor us, and provide a context for our own spiritual stories.

Anna exists within the culture and faith tradition of her times. She also exists as the grandmother archetype. She demonstrates how the experiences of her long life give her a heightened inner awareness. She uses her inner wisdom skillfully. She realizes that sometimes it is best just to be present, receptive and grateful, rather than expend a lot of energy with words. In some traditions, such as Zen Buddhism, there is a state of consciousness referred to as "robai-shin" or "Grandmother Mind." In the thirteenth century, Eihei Dogen, founder of the Soto School, gave the instruction to his students to develop the qualities of "Grandmother Mind." He said, "You cannot go beyond your abilities and your intelligence unless you have robai-shin, Grandmother Mind, the mind of great compassion. This compassion must help all of humanity. You should not think only of yourself."[43] Although this tenderness can be activated through our connection to our biological grandchildren, it is also a certain quality of the heart without regard to our families, gender, or age. This is an all-encompassing love symbolized in the deep connection between a young child and a much older person. The innocent child, the precious newborn, awakens the expansive love of Grandmother Heart. This is unlike any other kind of love we have ever experienced. Grandmother Mind and Heart hold all children in an interconnected web of life. The earth and its creatures are caught in this diamond net of heartstrings. There is hope in this kind of love that runs deep. Within this wisdom awareness, the heart expresses itself without self-consciousness and without conditions. This love is a floodlight revealing that care for the earth and all its children is the way, the clear calling, and hope for the future. Anna, Grandmother Heart, is an expression of selfless love coming up to meet the future with reverence, gratitude, and a vision of hope.

REFLECTIONS & QUESTIONS

1. There are times that call for outpourings of lavish verbal expressions and praise. There are also times for grateful recognition for which there are few words.

   Think about times when you have expressed each of these states. Reflect on how they are similar and the subtleties of how we experience them as different.

2. Joseph Campbell said that when we hold onto to old religious or traditional beliefs, we run the risk of missing significant spiritual experiences altogether because they don't fit our image of an experience of God.

   What is your reaction to Campbell's statement? Can you think of the times you have experienced this or observed when this has been true?

3. Age brings with it the advantage of perspective.
   How do you notice this perspective of age in your own life? What are the benefits of aging for you? How do you honor and respect the wisdom of years in yourself and in others you know or have known? What ancestral wisdom do you honor and appreciate?

4. Grandmother Mind and Heart is the expansion of caring that is unconditional and inclusive. It is something anyone can open to and express.
   How does the wisdom of age contribute to the experience and expression of Grandmother Heart? What is its significance and potential?

Ruth Ann Lonardelli

5. We are all aware of male wisdom teachers and sages. Most people are unaware of the many ways women have contributed to our spiritual heritage and to the development of civilization.
What were you specifically taught about powerful women in your cultural history? Can you identify any female characters from history who have inspired you?

Hearing Her Voice:
This Is My Son,
Whom I Love!

J *ohn said to the crowds coming out to be baptized by him,*
"You brood of vipers! Who warned you to flee from the
coming wrath? Produce fruit in keeping with repentance....
The ax is already at the root of the trees, and every tree that
does not produce good fruit will be cut down and thrown into
the fire.... Anyone who has two tunics should share with him
who has none, and the one who has food should do the same....
I baptize you with water. But one more powerful than I will
come, the thongs of whose sandals I am not worthy to untie...."

When all the people were being baptized, Jesus was bap-
tized too. And as he was praying, heaven was opened and the
Holy Spirit descended on him in bodily form like a dove...."
And a voice came from heaven: "You are my Son, whom I
love; with you I am well pleased."

LUKE 3:7-8A, 9, 11, 16A, 21-22 (NIV)

THE RIVER JORDAN FLOWS IN A CIRCUITOUS ROUTE FROM
the Sea of Galilee to the Dead Sea. It meanders through the

narrowest slips of the Great Rift Valley and plunges into the lowest river descent in the world. Rain and melting snow from Mount Hermon feed the streams that nourish its waters. At times, the river crosses terrain that varies in elevation by nearly 800 feet. It winds through lush tropical vegetation into sparse, rugged passageways and though dry, sandy hills. In some areas willows gracefully arch across the river dipping their fronds into the water's surface. Dense thickets of reeds sprout up at the river's edge. In other spots, steep, rocky, treacherous slopes can make river access impossible, but there are also places where a person can easily walk through scrawny patches of mustard plants to sandy beaches.

John, "the baptizer," and a group of his followers can often be found camping at one of these sandy beaches. At times, large crowds gather to hear him speak. John's approach is simple and direct. He is powerfully driven by his disgust for political corruption and religious laxity. On a cool overcast morning, small fires can be seen dotting the riverside where John and his friends huddle together for warmth. Dressed in a coarse tunic, John sits, resting with the others, waiting for daybreak. The sky lightens and he rises to speak. The others rise, too, oblivious to the morning chill. John starts out softly at first, affectionately greeting some of his most loyal followers. Then swaying a bit, as if to gain momentum, he begins: "Brood of vipers!" His voice rings out startling the birds nesting in the reeds. He is railing against lax religious practices, challenging the people to supplant rote obedience to the laws with genuine devotion to God, and to resist the corruption of the political and religious leaders. He is warning them of coming wrath and prodding them to prepare for the end times and turn away from their sinful past and repent. He is admonishing them to care for others and tend to the needs of strangers.

Jesus stands among them. He has heard John's message so many times he can almost predict each word. John's boisterous prophecies and pronouncements resonate throughout Jesus' blood and bones. John is the first to throw off his clothes and step into the water. Then, one by one they all cast aside their clothing and move toward the chilly Jordan River to be baptized. For the followers of John, this ritual represents a death to their past life and readiness for a new beginning—a turning away from the past toward the future.

Some of them immerse fully. Others step out into the waters where they stand or kneel while John pours the water onto their heads. Jesus is the last to enter the river. He also removes his robe, sinking to his knees in prayer. Perhaps he lowers himself fully into the flowing Jordan River. In whatever way he enters into this ritual, he will walk away from it changed. When the ritual comes to a close, the morning clouds part and a clear shaft of sunlight shines onto the newly baptized. Beads of water on their bodies catch the sun's rays and glisten jewel-like. Shivering, speechless, their attention turns to a miraculous sight. Out of nowhere, a snowy white dove appears gliding in the clear morning sky. As it flutters above Jesus' head, the voice of Divine Love calls out, "This is my son, whom I love." All of his knowledge, study, and preparation have brought him to this moment of re-emergence, of rebirth into the awareness of this immense love and his divine purpose. There is still more interior work to do, but his calling is now clear, and although his work parallels John's ministry, their paths will soon diverge.

Water rituals are among the oldest and most common observances in religious cultures around the world. Centuries before John the Baptist was baptizing in the River Jordan, water rituals were being performed by the Zoroastrians.[44] In the Middle East and among Hindus in India, ritual bathing in the Ganges is still thought to wash away sin and karma. In ancient Egypt, water from the Nile was believed to possess restorative qualities and provide spiritual cleansing. The baptism of newborn children was routinely performed to purify them from the birth process. In Roman culture, at the time of Jesus and generations before, ritual purification was carried out by the Mithrains, whose stories precede and closely parallel those of Jesus.[45] Over the centuries, the Hebrews have performed the *mikvah* bath— an observance that covers a wide range of purposes, from consecration to purification. For the ancient Celts, immersion miraculously restored fallen warriors to life. Elaborate ceremonies, strict laws, customs, and preparations developed around many of these observances.[46] Whether the purpose was to bless, purify, or extend ablution, there are the transcultural, timeless implications that water rituals suggest: renewal, rejuvenation, cleansing of the sins of the flesh, rebirth, and spiritual transformation.

The symbolism of baptism must have been blatantly obvious in a culture in which it held such prominence. Professor Ron Moseley noted, "The baptismal water (Mikveh) in rabbinic literature was referred to as the womb of the world.... As the convert came out of these waters his status was changed and he was referred to as 'a little child just born.'"[47]

The symbolic language of spiritual renewal and transformation comes primarily from the feminine experience.

Terms such as "birth" and "rebirth" mark stages of break-through awareness. The baptismal waters cleanse us, renew us, and with womb-like, mysterious properties, prepare us for new life. As Erich Neumann wrote in his classic, *The Great Mother,* "Wherever we encounter the symbol of rebirth, we have to do with a matriarchal transformation mystery, and *this is true even when its symbolism or inter-pretation bears a patriarchal disguise.*"[48]

Death and resurrection were the prevailing narratives of the agricultural cultures of the goddess. The mystery of nature played out in planting practices and harvesting ritu-als. The seed, the physical form, breaks open so new life can germinate. It is planted within the earth—the dark mystery of the tomb. It is here that transformation happens and the earth becomes the generative womb bringing forth new life. Christian culture, in which patriarchy has reigned, is full of many stories and rituals with similar themes. Death, resurrection, and spiritual rebirth figure prominently. Other activities commonly associated with the feminine recur throughout the gospel stories. Little children are welcomed. Meals are served. People gather together to share food and to celebrate at weddings. They are healed. Through the everyday common, practical concerns of life lived on Earth, spiritual lessons are revealed. Symbolism more commonly equated with the masculine is less evident in the gospel stories. The Jesus stories do not usually use metaphors of the powerful, of kings and warriors, battles or sports, to illustrate a spiritual message. Swords have been put away. Instead, seeds are scattered, planted and harvested, and there are lilies growing in the fields.

Standing as witnesses to this scene by the River Jordan, we behold the feminine face of God. Here, at the River of

Life, is an ancient reenactment of rebirth and transformation. Jesus experiences rebirth in the enactment of baptism. When he arises from the waters, he is arising into a new level of consciousness—a transformative, unitive shift into expanded spiritual awareness. At that moment, "The Holy Spirit descended on him in bodily form like a dove."

The dove was widely recognized as a symbol of the mother goddess in the ancient civilizations of Crete and Sumer. It also appeared in Roman mythology and was associated with the goddess of love Aphrodite. As the symbol of the dove was integrated into the religion of the Hebrews, it retained feminine qualities. The dove was associated with the feminine Hebrew word for spirit: *ruach*, Holy Spirit known as the indwelling spirit of God. It seems to be fitting that the feminine face of the divine would show up in this story of spiritual transformation in the form of the dove and the great, compassionate mother voice: "This is my son, whom I love." Jesus receives the added blessing and assurance of his deep connection to Mother God, the regenerative source of compassion, healing, and wisdom.

This story contains two key symbols representative of the Divine Feminine. Water, which is symbolic of the amniotic fluid of birth and renewal, and the dove, associated with the Sacred Feminine, come together and initiate Jesus into the wisdom path. Sophia, the Greek name for wisdom, appears in the Hebrew tradition as an aspect of the sacred. She appears in the form of the descending dove. She recognizes, affirms, and blesses the embodiment of life in the world. In this scene, in this simple natural setting along the Jordan River, as Jesus rises from the waters, she claims him as her beloved son. "Sophia symbolizes the Divine

Feminine, the 'web of life' that characterizes the world of nature, and the presence of the divine within the human soul, which yearns for mystical union."[49] In being baptized, Jesus is initiated as a wisdom teacher, the embodiment of Sophia.

REFLECTIONS & QUESTIONS

1. Special moments that seem imbued with sacred meaning mark our spiritual transformation and awakening.
   What moments of sacred meaning have been indicators of a shift in your spiritual awareness? What community events have you participated in that have marked transformative moments in your life or the lives of others?

2. Water is a powerful symbol, and it evokes strong memories and feelings.
   What are some of the ways that water evokes feelings in you?

3. Water is an essential element in our daily lives. It is the source that nurtures us, sustains us, and creates life.
   How do you honor and respect water on a daily basis? What are some aspects of renewal in your everyday activities involving water?

Facing the Shadow: The Wilderness

Then Jesus was led by the Spirit into the wilderness to be tempted by the devil. After fasting forty days and forty nights, he was hungry. The tempter came to him and said, "If you are the Son of God, tell these stones to become bread."

Jesus answered, "It is written: 'Man shall not live on bread alone, but on every word that comes from the mouth of God.'"

Then the devil took him to the holy city and had him stand on the highest point of the temple. "If you are the Son of God," he said, "throw yourself down...."

Jesus answered him. "Do not put the Lord your God to the test."

Again, the devil took him to a very high mountain and showed him all the kingdoms of the world and their splendor. "All this I will give you," he said, "if you will bow down and worship me."

Jesus said to him, "Away from me, Satan! For it is written: 'Worship the Lord your God, and serve him only.'"

Then the devil left him, and angels came and attended him.

MATTHEW 4:1-6A,7-11 (NIV)

THE DESERT OF JUDEA RISES IN BARE CRAGS AND FALLS into flat plains. Compacted layers of windblown sediment, dispersed in volcanic activity eons ago, have settled into irregular cliffs. Erosion from scouring winds has etched overhangs and caves in the cliff sides. Pulverized grit and rock form the desert floor. During the day, the sun bears down with a relentless glare. The earth seems to throb from the heat. In the distance, the light, the air, and the heat mingle, spinning illusions. Forms and shapes seem to move across the landscape. They pace, stretch, and spin away into nothingness. The nights are fiercely cold. Stars pierce the darkness with startling clarity. They seem to be layered from the brightest to a luminous thumbprint smearing across the sky. Silence, welcome at first, takes on an intrusive presence, like a guest who stays too long. An occasional animal call momentarily scatters the quietness, but the quiet quickly returns, covering over the echoes with its broad sweep.

A slight figure stirs on the horizon. Who would be out here alone? Look closer. It appears to be a man. By our standards, he is small. No more than 5 feet 2 inches tall; no heavier than 110 pounds. Why would anyone want to be here in this wild and rugged, dangerous landscape? There is no water, not a stream or a trickle anywhere. Nothing appears edible or sustaining. The man has brought no provisions with him. Who comes here but someone who is lost? A madman? An outcast?

We are told he came here to be alone. Where might you go to be alone? To a place like this? I might find a cottage by the sea, a place of gentle reflection. Not this spiritual teacher. He has been traveling throughout the countryside, meeting people, preaching, stopping to teach and heal. Even as demanding as his work is, he sets aside the cries for help and healing to follow a rich vein of wisdom to deep introspection. He knows he will need to go within, dig deeper, and this time of deep inner reflection requires a quiet place apart from the distractions of everyday life. He understands the importance of this interior work. In the Gospel of Thomas, the teacher, Jesus, is quoted, "If you will not know yourselves, you dwell in poverty and it is you who are that poverty."[50]

There are no distractions here. Not in this lonely, sparse landscape. No distractions except basic survival itself—hunger and thirst. No distractions but the mind spinning a specter of inner dramas. First, recycling the events of the last few days and all the people with their problems and stories. He reconstructs the fragments of conversations and complaints: the painful memories, the taunts of playmates, and the misunderstanding of family. He feels the loneliness of being different and the what if's: What might he have said? What might he have done? Forty days and forty nights—a number symbolizing completion or maturity—is a long time, long enough to play out intricate dramas on the mind's stage. Ego appears in the chorus of deprecating internal voices. Just WHO do you think you are? Who made you GOD? What makes you think YOU know anything?

Then ego takes an inflated form: See how strong you are! How powerful you are! You can have it all! Power! Dominion over all things! Riches! It seems so real, as if it has a presence all its own. Ego expressed as imagination plays out a fantasy of accolades, the adoring crowds, the honors and praise. He is present to a vertiginous temptation to flex his supernatural muscle and throw himself into an abyss. You are invincible! You'll fly! You'll defy the laws of gravity! You will be on top of the world! Yes! Go ahead!

Perhaps he laughs out loud and shakes his head at the inner spectacle. Maybe he follows one or two or more trails of thought and becomes caught in their crevices but then pulls himself out. Perhaps he chants or sings to cover the sound of the voices, or shouts at the chattering phantoms puncturing his peace.

Many of us are familiar with the Sunday School interpretation of this story. An external force, Satan, is confronted and subdued. This makes a compelling story; however, in some ways it is a tragic misunderstanding. Such thinking demonizes and projects an external entity, missing an opportunity for deep, profound spiritual transformation. A more meaningful understanding allows that Jesus confronts and subdues the interior energies, the ego, the shadow thoughts that taunt and tempt us all. These mental states, notes Rev. Eric Butterworth, are "...the inertial pull of limited states of consciousness resisting the upward reach of man's higher aspirations."[51] Challenging this interior world is the work necessary for anyone who wants to live an authentic spiritual life. Facing these mental states transforms them into our teachers. We come to understand our shadow as less about how sinful we are and our personal struggles with inherent darkness, and more about the stirrings of conscience. Darkness provides the contrast for illumination to come forth. When we awaken to the stirrings of the sacred within us we also become increasingly aware of our human weakness and failings.

For forty days and nights, in this time apart, Jesus witnesses the inner struggles and self-destructive thoughts seeking to divert him from fulfilling his mission. In this profound interior, the stark landscape of the soul, he accepts the challenge of facing everything it means to struggle with the dark side of being human. He undergoes a process that evokes the true nature of this brilliant, beloved teacher and prepares him for the work ahead. The story concludes with Jesus' recognition of the shadow self. He names it, releases it, and puts it behind him. "Away from me, Satan," he says, as he affirms his intention to "worship and serve" God only.

Similar stories appear in other traditions, as well. Buddha also endures a period of temptation and inner struggle under the Bodhi tree before obtaining enlightenment. Buddha, like Jesus, is tempted to turn away from his spiritual path. He is bombarded by images of whirling demons, yet the Buddha's resolve also holds and his trickster mind is subdued.

Jesus and Buddha recognized the importance of serious introspection and confronting the shadow. Both emerge from their respective experiences ready to bring their teaching to the world. Sufi teacher Llewellyn Vaughan-Lee said, "This psychological work is essential, for example, working with the shadow, the darkness within ourselves.... If you don't work on them, they can subvert the whole spiritual process...."[52] In the Buddhist tradition, and in some Judeo-Christian practices, there is a belief that doing psychological self-reflection grows spiritual qualities such as wisdom, patience, tolerance, generosity, and compassion. Buddha and Jesus exemplify the enlightened, higher Self. In their shadow work, the personal ego (the little self) eventually breaks open to birth a selfless, integrated Self, and a new capacity emerges to bridge the divide between the conscious and unconscious. Carl Jung called this the "God-image," the archetype of wholeness, the ordering principle that serves to unify and center our interior worlds.[53]

Ruth Ann Lonardelli

The God-image Jesus demonstrates is the sacred essence within our ordinary experiences. This is the "real life" realm of the Mother, the dark humus which breaks down old structures in order to birth the new.

Jesus does not make a distinction between the spiritual and the psychological. They are both part of the one essence. He emerges with all the distractions of patriarchal power subdued. In the version from Matthew, the next time we hear much about him, Jesus is delivering one of the most well-known and beautiful of all spiritual teachings: the Sermon on the Mount. In this, Jesus gives the gift of supreme blessings—the beatitudes—the first and one of the most beloved of all his teachings.

The Sermon on the Mount and subsequent passages is a series of affirmative prayers and practical advice. In this address, Jesus speaks to the integrated awareness of the psychological, emotional, and spiritual aspects of our humanness. This is timeless, inspirational teaching. He demonstrates the spirit of feminine consciousness in which the most basic experiences of life are imbued with the sacred. "Blessed are the poor in spirit…. Blessed are the peacemakers." Our spirits are revived. We are comforted. Blessed. These teachings are followed by tough love, which is straightforward and unequivocal: whatever our grudges and victim stories, get over it. Make peace with our adversary, clean up our language, love our enemies, and accept responsibility for our actions.

This is the great spiritual work to be done. We will go through our own wilderness experience on the path to higher consciousness. Extraordinary teachers show us the way through these challenges by their example. They demonstrate that we can confront what is within us *without identifying with it.* We are able to observe and witness what comes up in us without fixating on it, and *without projecting* it onto others. We can put these things behind us and move into a fuller realization of our life purpose. Then all of our inner specters will vanish like vapors, as we follow our Christ nature, our Buddha nature, which is at the very heart of Spirit.

REFLECTIONS & QUESTIONS

1. After experiencing a radical spiritual shift, it is not uncommon to enter a time some call "the dark night of the soul." This difficult time might lead us into an even deeper understanding of who we are.
   In what ways can you relate to Jesus' wilderness experience?

2. In this wilderness of the mind, our thoughts rise up to meet us in surprising and disturbing ways. At some point, we need to recognize that although we have these thoughts, they do not define us.
   How can the realization we are more than our thoughts help us in observing them without being swept away by their seductive power?

3. Jesus and Buddha demonstrate the importance of this interior work and how to live with this critical process. They do so by recognizing the importance of facing the shadow sides of ourselves, acknowledging the power of our thoughts, letting them have their say without identifying with them, and challenging these states by setting boundaries for how long we listen to them.
   What are some ways you have moved through your own challenging, wilderness experiences? What value have you found in your "dark night of the soul"?

Severing Higher Consciousness: Herod

*N*ow Herod had arrested John and bound him and
put him in prison because of Herodias, his brother
Philip's wife, for John had been saying to him, "It is
not lawful for you to have her."

Herod wanted to kill John, but he was afraid of the people,
because they considered John a prophet.

On Herod's birthday, the daughter of Herodias danced
for the guests and pleased Herod, so much that he promised
with an oath to give her whatever she asked.

Prompted by her mother, she said, "Give me here on a
platter the head of John the Baptist."

The king was distressed, but because of his oaths and his
dinner guests, he ordered that her request be granted and
had John beheaded in the prison. His head was brought in on
a platter and given to the girl, who carried it to her mother.

MATT 14: 3-11 (NIV)

HEROD HAS HIS TROUBLES WITH JOHN. CROWDS FIND
the wild prophet irresistible. He is a ridiculous sight, dressed
in a sparse, coarse tunic—it is no more than a wide swath

of cloth that flares open when he walks. His dark eyes flash a deep, embedded blaze. John's voice booms with passion. He commands attention with his bold pronouncements.

Crowds make Herod nervous, especially when they gather to hear condemnation of power and privilege, rather than to praise rulers such as him. Added to this are John's strange, troubling messages about mysterious, supernatural events and dire predictions. Herod cannot see any good to come from this. Things get too personal when his own private life, including his questionable marriage to his sister-in-law Herodias, becomes the subject of John's ravings. How dare this wild, nearly naked, unseemly, loud, and raucous character disparage him, Herod, the ruler of Galilee?

Herod wants John dead, but he is not without his sensibilities. He would prefer nothing distract from his birthday celebration. It is a grand party. Wine flows, the food so abundant it overflows from the table top into baskets onto the floor. Herod is heartened by the cheerfulness of the event, relieved from brooding over his troubles by the party mood of his guests, and he relishes the attention. He registers the awe his company shows for the generous feast and the colorful and amusing entertainment. Besotted by the wine and glowing with self-appreciation, he is easily carried away by a young dancer. Salome twirls and dips, lunges and leaps, whipping her veil in artful seductive sweeps. His applause is heard above all the others. He brings the young dancer forward, and, in front of the guests, promises to give her whatever she wants. The girl does not want to waste this request on anything frivolous. She imagines a wardrobe of fine garments, a beautiful house on a hilltop, her own servant to tend to her needs. She runs to her mother, Herodias, for counsel. What transpires between them is a miserable disappointment. Surely there is a lively exchange of words—maternal threats and daughterly protests. After all, to ask for the severed head of a man she did not know—what could this possibly mean to a young woman? What does she care that John the Baptist voiced disapproval of her mother? He is not the only one.

Herodias grabs a platter from the table. Forcefully, she sends the young woman back to Herod with the request, "Give me here on a platter the head of John the Baptist." Herod blanches. Not here. Not now. A sober, heavy silence falls among the party guests. He can see the attention is turning away from him, from the party itself, to the wild prophet's fate. He did give his oath. Everyone heard his boastful, generous offer of granting a wish to the young woman asserting his kingly right of such dispensations. And, so it is done.

There is a little of Herod in all of us at some time in our lives. Herod's ego shows up as an over-inflated sense of self, a potentially violent defensiveness. His identity is dependent on approval from others. He demonstrates power by opposing another's ideas especially those ideas challenging the status quo or personal beliefs. His perverse sense of generosity is solely based on how he is perceived. His woundedness shows up as an addiction to being seen. When Herod holds a position of power in the community, he maintains his authority by fierce control. This is the only way he knows. When Herod holds a position of power in our lives, this figure can be resistant to any change that threatens our self-image or our desire to be in control. New ideas or ways of doing things are deeply troubling. Our internal Herods are distracted by our senses to the extent that we become either ineffectual or dangerous. The shallow allurement of our own young dancing girls—our undeveloped, immature unconscious states—show up as an addiction to watching television, shopping, surfing the Internet, or just about anything that dulls our perception.

Then there is Herodias. Her violent, vengeful rage exposes a dangerous perversion of creative energy and a disconnect with the generative power of the Sacred Feminine. Her volatile, impenetrable state prevails, deflecting self-knowledge and favoring deception. The union of Herod, and his inflated ego and unbridled force, with Herodias and her self-righteous, unconscious rage, is a dangerous one that precludes any access to wisdom and compassion. The beheading of John represents the complete severing of awareness and higher consciousness, as well as anything that challenges our self-serving ways. This is an extreme demonstration of rejecting the higher self for the lowest form of ego.

In spiritual terms, "the ego" refers to the way we maintain and adhere to a specific definition and image of our identity as defined by our roles, our stories, and our positions in society. Although this connects us to the activities of life, the problem arises from an over-identification with our roles and our stories to the exclusion of our authentic selves. This over-identification limits our responses to the challenges and opportunities that life presents. Like Herod, we become stuck in identifying with our predictable opinions and behaviors, even when they provide only inadequate responses to our life experiences—and even when it is apparent these ways of being no longer serve us. Yet this is all we know of who we are. No wonder we often succumb to feelings of dissatisfaction, disappointment, and self-defeating behavior. Everything we have attained and achieved can leave us wondering if we have overlooked something important. We might conclude, as did the Sufi mystic Rumi, "If you know the value of every article of merchandise but don't know the value of your own soul, it's all foolishness."[54]

Beneath the ego's thin veneer is our unrest. What is it? What is missing? We miss what we have forgotten. Fragments of memory lie just beneath the surface. We get a glimpse that nudges our consciousness into wakefulness, and we understand that at our deepest core all of our yearning is for creation itself—God (or whatever name you choose)—to know itself and be realized in expression through us, in us, as us. We are more than our personal stories, and yet this realization includes all of that, too. Yes, it is ineffable. Rooted deeply within us, we are the fields in which the life force itself pushes forth. It neither toils nor spins. But it is simply the sublime paradox of energy and stillness in which the particularities of our personalities blossom. And yet, like Herod, we settle for less. We become fixated on how we are seen, on power, position, and possessions, which leads us to severing our connection with what in Hinduism is called *Atman*—the true self beyond personal limitations.

REFLECTIONS & QUESTIONS

1. When an over-inflated ego-defensiveness holds power in our lives, there will also be strong internal opposition to self-awareness and self-responsibility. *What does being defensive mean to you? How would you describe what defensiveness feels like? How can we know the difference between feeling safe and being overly sensitive and defensive?*

2. The experiences of our senses add depth and joy to living. When we are distracted by shallow sensory experiences, we become cut off from our higher wisdom. We can become either ineffectual or dangerous. *How do we distinguish between shallow sensory experiences, which are alluring but ultimately unsatisfying, and the kinds of sensory experiences that are life-affirming? In what ways did Herod's pure enjoyment of Salome's dance become corrupted? What can we learn from this?*

Caring for Others in Troubling Times: Feeding the Five Thousand

John's disciples came and took his body and buried it. Then they went and told Jesus. When Jesus heard what had happened, he withdrew by boat privately to a solitary place. Hearing of this, the crowds followed him on foot from the towns. When Jesus landed and saw a large crowd, he had compassion on them and healed their sick.

As evening approached, the disciples came to him and said, "This is a remote place, and it's already getting late. Send the crowds away, so they can go to the villages and buy themselves some food." Jesus replied, "They do not need to go away. You give them something to eat." "We have here only five loaves of bread and two fishes," they answered. "Bring them here to me," he said. And he directed the people to sit down on the grass. Taking the five loaves and the two fish and looking up to heaven, he gave thanks and broke the loaves. Then he gave them to the disciples, and the disciples gave them to the people. They all ate and were satisfied, and the disciples picked up twelve basketfuls of broken pieces that were left over. The number of those who ate was about five thousand men, besides women and children.

MATTHEW 14:12-21 (NIV)

Ruth Ann Lonardelli

JESUS RECEIVES THE MESSAGE A LITTLE BEFORE SUNRISE, just as the hills are coming into view. A soft, dim light is spreading across the Galilean sky. The first thing he sees that morning, laying on his back on the ground, are the birds, still shadowy in the darkness, lifting above the lake and rising toward the far shore. He is sitting up, fully awake, looking off into the pale pink hills when they arrive. The women and men who had been with John in his ministry gather around Jesus weeping. They bring him news of John's death.

The shock and grief are keenly felt. An ache so real it catches in the throat. A tight knot of grief settles in his chest. Jesus has known John since childhood. As young boys, they ran through the hills and splashed in the water near where the mourners now gather. John and Jesus spent many nights under the stars, marveling at the vastness of the skies and exploring questions about life and God. John had been his teacher, his inspiration, and his friend. Wordlessly, Jesus turns to the others and they hold each other as they weep. In a flash, he experiences the human propensity to question, to doubt, colliding with his own sense of a higher purpose. Could he have done something to spare John from such a fate? After all, he had saved others—why could he not save John?

Jesus longs for a quiet place to be alone with his grief. He moves away and slips into a boat and pushes off from shore for a secluded spot on the mountainside. He is seeking solitude to think, to pray, and reflect on his loss, but a crowd from the village is gathering. They follow him—the curious, the crippled, and the enchanted. They gather on the shore, and when Jesus sees the people and their concerns he puts aside his own grief and turns to them. "He had compassion on them and healed their sick."

In his book *Creating True Peace*, the Buddhist monk Thich Nhat Hanh writes, "Do not think that because you are suffering you can speak harshly, retaliate or punish others. You can still help others as you embrace the suffering inside you."[55]

The Great Compassionate Heart of God is at work in Jesus. Just as an attentive, loving mother stops in the midst of her own concerns and tends to the needs of others, Jesus teaches us the way through our loss is to serve. He does not entirely forego his time of private grief. He will attend to this at another time. He understands his own needs, but he also has compassion for the needs of others.

For those who are gathered, it seems a timeless day, as if they are suspended in eternity in the sunlit countryside. The people listen in rapt attention to the teachings. Exclamations and murmurs ripple through the crowd as they witness the healings. Some of them see the landscape, the horizon, the sky, and the faces of their loved ones for the first time. Others are walking without assistance. Some hear the sounds of laughter and the cries of children.

Soon other material and physical demands of life become pressing concerns. The disciples bring them to Jesus' attention. This is all good—the teaching and healing—but it is getting late. Soon it will be dark. The people need to eat, so it would be best to send them away.

Rather than sending the crowd away for food, Jesus tells the disciples to give them what they have. Such a ridiculous paltry amount of food is all they can provide—five loaves

Ruth Ann Lonardelli

of bread, two fish. It would take a magic trick, a miracle, to transform the small amount into enough to feed over 5,000 people. But it is no more than the miracle Mother Earth demonstrates when she takes in a handful of grain to produce a harvest of abundance.

When we become focused on the miraculous in this drama, we neglect each step in the process. Slowing down the pace of this story and carefully following each sequential gesture gives us some valuable insights into how not having enough can turn into an experience of abundance. "Taking up the five loaves and two fish and looking up to heaven, he gave thanks...." What had seemed daunting was, in truth, such a simple thing: *all it had taken was bringing forth what they already had, raising it up to heaven—into higher awareness—and giving thanks.*

Sometimes it appears that all we have is so small, such a little bit and so very ordinary. Sometimes there seems so little in us to share; however, in Christ consciousness nothing is lacking. Jesus lifts up the food and looks toward heaven, but he is not praying for some external god to intervene. Spiritual teacher Charles Fillmore wrote, "Prayer is more than asking God for help in the physical world; it is in its highest sense the opening up in our soul of an innate spiritual umbilical cord that connects us with the Holy Mother, from which we can receive a perpetual flow of life."[56]

As Jesus looks up, his attention focuses inward. He is accessing an internal state of direct contact with his spiritual source. In some Buddhist and Yoga traditions, this state is known as "higher consciousness." With this awareness comes a sense of oneness, a union of the transcendent and the immanent. To paraphrase twentieth century mystic

Joel Goldsmith, we are within the wholeness of God, and the wholeness of God is within us.[57] Like the attraction of gravity, this force is always there for us. When we align our attention with the gravitational pull of our spiritual nature, we find ourselves responding to perceived needs with an outpouring of generosity. It has been speculated that when the disciples brought forth their loaves and fishes these served to prime the pump of shared resources. It seems unlikely that a group of people would have come to such a gathering without bringing their own provisions. When they all brought forth their own portions to share there was an abundance of food to fulfill everyone's need to overflowing. It was a miracle of the awakened human heart.

Christ consciousness is the experience of all-embracing universal compassion in the broadest sense, while also sensing deep empathy and appreciation for the smallest and most mundane aspects of life. When we look at the example of Jesus, we see the inner, deeper meaning of looking up and inward as a centering gesture connecting us to the spiritual reality within us. The kingdom is within, expansive, creative, and complete.[58] This is a boundless, generous state of nonduality, of oneness, and it is so full that scarcity and separation become non-existent.

How are we to gain access to this higher consciousness, this kingdom of heaven? As this story reveals, the catalyst can be as humble and ordinary as five loaves of bread and two fish. We need only be present to whatever is before us and approach it with beginner's mind—curiosity without preconceived notions of how it is supposed to be.

Jesus demonstrates the most fundamental practice that shows up again and again in these spiritual stories. Giving thanks ignites the process. Jesus is giving thanks as if those needs *are* already fulfilled. When we are *truly grateful for what we already have, despite appearances, and resist the temptation to focus on what seems to be missing,* we become more aware of the resources available to us. Jesus knows the alchemical power of thanksgiving has the mysterious ability to change everything. Praise is not something we do for God or to appease some cosmic deity. God is not in need of our thanks. We express thanksgiving in order to enter into a deeper experience of connection and bliss. When we do so, a miracle does happen. In some inexplicable way, even the air we breathe seems infused with radiance, the cells of our bodies humming a chorus of hallelujahs. Blessings follow such practices. "They all ate and were satisfied."

The late afternoon sun is leaning into dusk, and Jesus knows that if the crowd does not disperse quickly, they will not arrive at their homes before dark. He directs his disciples to board their boat and take off for the opposite shore. He will meet them later. He understands that when the people see him leave, they will begin to scatter. He tells them it is time to go home. Now, finally, Jesus can seek refuge and rest in prayer and solitude. He has the wisdom and compassion to change his plans and tend to the needs of those before him, *but he also has not forgotten his own needs.* "He went up on a mountainside by himself to pray. When evening came, he was there alone." On the mountain, an elevated state, symbolizing ascended consciousness, he prays, meditates, and renews his connection with his Sacred Source.

REFLECTIONS & QUESTIONS

1. The way through our own losses is to turn to the needs of others.
   How has serving others helped you to gain perspective on your own problems?

2. Although we might be flexible about when and where to find time for our own healing and restorative work, we need to make certain we rest and renew ourselves.
   How do you factor in renewal time? How do you feel if you need to reschedule renewal time? What do you experience when you do not make time for yourself?

3. The alchemical power of thanksgiving has the mysterious ability to change everything.
   What do you think this statement means? What kind of sensory state accompanies thankfulness, and what role does such a state play in the process of change?

4. In this story, we learn three things to help us access a higher state of consciousness. First, there is mental openness or beginners' mind. Second is the recognition of what is available rather than focusing on what is lacking. Third is the expression of thanksgiving for what we already have.
   Reflect on these three points and how they relate to your own experience. How do you think they are helpful? What is your experience of higher/Christ consciousness?

The Lotus:
Walking on Water

J esus made the disciples get into the boat and go on ahead of
him to the other side, while he dismissed the crowd. After
he had dismissed them, he went up on a mountainside
by himself to pray. Later that night he was there alone, but
the boat was already a considerable distance from land, buffeted by the waves because the wind was against it. Shortly
before dawn Jesus went out to them, walking on the lake.
When the disciples saw him walking on the lake, they were
terrified. "It's a ghost," they said, and cried out in fear. But
Jesus immediately said to them: "Take courage! It is I. Don't
be afraid. "Lord, if it is you," Peter replied, "tell me to come
to you on the water." "Come," he said. Then Peter got down
out of the boat, walked on the water and came toward Jesus.
But when he saw the wind, he was afraid, and, beginning to
sink, cried out, "Lord, save me!" Immediately Jesus reached
out his hand and caught him. "You of little faith," he said,
"why did you doubt?" And when they climbed into the boat,
the wind died down.

MATTHEW 14:22-32 (NIV)

Earlier in the day Jesus set off for the mountain-side alone. So much was on his heart, and he longed for some peace, a quiet place to pray, meditate and listen for inner guidance. He made it only as far as the boat that would take him to the mountain across the lake. So many had gathered to hear him. Some had come from far away. They carried their own burdens, and some carried their family and friends. Many of them longed for spiritual peace, for comfort from their fears. He had compassion for all of them. All day he taught them, blessed them, comforted them, and healed them. Then, at the end of the day, he sent the crowd home. The people would need to return to their homes before it became too dark to find their way safely across the rocky hills. Jesus instructed his disciples to use one of the boats and head for the far shore. He would join them later on the other side. Then he went alone on the mountain, a place above the fray, an elevated state, where he prayed and meditated.

"When evening came he was there alone...." Evening is the threshold between two worlds sometimes referred to as "liminal time," when our personal identities meet the world of spirit. This is a time of transition out of the day's concerns and our daytime roles into night's deep rest. Mountain-sides are physical spaces representing this meeting ground between realms—not the very pinnacle, but a place lifted up above the world, yet still within Earth's range. This is sacred territory, a place of peace and rest in which we can release the expectations of family, friends, and work, a place to be in the silence and return to our sacred source. At this point, our humanness reconnects with our spiritual center. For Jesus, this time and place in the mountains renews his spirit and his connection with pure Christ essence.

Meanwhile, the disciples in the boat never reach the other shore. Most are experienced seamen. All of them live close to nature, and they certainly know the signs of an impending storm. We do not know why they do not arrive at the other shore before the storm breaks. They are already a considerable distance from land when they are buffeted by the waves. Our journey through life can be like this. Even when we have a clear sense of direction and know exactly where we are headed, we can become overwhelmed by circumstances. Once again we are caught in fear, anxiety, and worry. In the company of others who are also afraid, our concerns intensify.

At first they think they are seeing a ghost. Then they see Jesus coming toward them. He is walking on the water. It is a startling sight. Peter represents the limitations of our human reach when we put our newly acquired spiritual knowledge to the test only to find ourselves less advanced than we had hoped. He expresses his desire to walk on water, too. Jesus invites Peter to join him. "Come on," Jesus says. Peter gets out of the boat and stands on the watery surface for a moment before becoming self-conscious and afraid. Then he begins to sink. Jesus reaches down, lifts him up, and helps him back into the boat. The two of them climb in together and the storm is subdued, the waters calmed.

If we take this story literally, Jesus has performed a miracle. He has defied natural laws. Similar miracle stories exist in other traditions. Buddha appeared levitating over the water some 500 years before Jesus. Levitation and defying natural laws are part of the tradition of miracles and supernatural phenomena. These stories can be taken literally, or they can be seen as more than literal. That is, as stories revealing timeless, universal spiritual truths.

In the Hindu and Buddhist traditions, the lotus is a symbol of spiritual awakening. Its roots go down deep beneath the waters and into the primal soup of life. The stem rises up through the muck and mire, passing through the moving current, breaking the surface into the radiant sunshine. The flower bud unfolds its pure, fragrant petals and floats peacefully above the water, basking in the sunlight. The pristine blossom reaches upward, sometimes as much as 8-12 inches, drifting and swaying gracefully, regardless of the churned up condition of the waters below. This lotus symbol represents the ascension of consciousness rising up from the cloudy amniotic waters of generation, through the shifting currents of our thoughts and emotions and reaching up toward the light, into illumination and enlightenment.

In Eastern art, pictures of the lotus blossom often include depictions of Brahma, the Hindu god of creation or some other deity. In Buddhism, the Buddha, peacefully centered and cradled in the lotus blossom, radiates sublime peacefulness and tranquility. The Buddha serenely floats above the water.

Jesus appearing to the disciples as he walks across the stormy waves represents a similar peaceful, enlightened consciousness. He has rooted and centered himself in prayer and meditation. He is now capable of rising above the shifting currents of thoughts and emotions. He is skimming the top of the dark troubled waters of the lake like the serene and triumphant lotus. Jesus, like the lotus, symbolizes a peaceful presence in the midst of instability. Peter, representing our less evolved state of consciousness, wants to be as centered as Jesus, but he is tossed around in a boat full of worries, concerns, and fears. Peter is not able to sustain a peaceful presence and he sinks. Yet the possibility exists—the invitation is open—and one day he might be able to transcend the circumstances of the storm. This story demonstrates, in its more than literal meaning, that this possibility also exists for us.

One day we might be in a place of riding the waves of unrest like the lotus, skimming the surface tension of our world. Although we might not be there yet, and we are not quite ready, the peaceful presence of Christ consciousness, which connects and holds us all, gets into the boat with us, comes to us in our humanness in order to settle us and calm our storms.

REFLECTIONS & QUESTIONS

1. When we feel restored and reconnected with our
    spiritual source, we are able to ride the waves of
    unrest in our lives.
    *What spiritual practices help you in dealing with the
    tensions of the world? What else might you add or do
    to assist in staying deeply grounded?*

2. In the company of others who are also afraid, our
    concerns intensify.
    *How does the company you keep affect your own
    emotional experience?*

3. Even if we are not there yet, and perhaps we
    overestimate our spiritual progress, the power and
    presence of Spirit meets us where we are.
    *Imagine being calm and experiencing a sense of deep-
    rooted connection with your spiritual source when
    you are faced with difficulties in your life.*

Ruth Ann Lonardelli

Everyone is a Teacher:
The Canaanite Woman

Jesus...went to the vicinity of Tyre. He entered a house and did not want anyone to know it; yet he could not keep his presence a secret. In fact, as soon as she heard about him, a woman whose little daughter was possessed by an evil spirit came and fell at his feet. The woman was a Greek, born in Syrian Phoenicia. She begged Jesus to drive the demon out of her daughter. "First let the children eat all they want," he told her, "for it is not right to take the children's bread and toss it to the dogs." "Yes, Lord," she replied, "but even the dogs under the table eat the children's crumbs." Then he told her, "For such a reply, you may go; the demon has left your daughter," She went home and found her child lying on the bed, and the demon gone.

MARK 7:25-30 (NIV)

JESUS IS IN UNFAMILIAR TERRITORY IN TYRE, WHICH IS on the outer edges of where he has traveled before, both geographically and in awareness. He enters a house with the hope his presence will be kept a secret. Unlike the stories of a Jesus who willingly attends to the needs of others, here he demonstrates the humanness of the contracted heart. He does not merely seek rest; he wishes to restrict his dealings with the people of Tyre—those outside his tribe. Jesus is about to encounter a situation leading to a breakthrough in his understanding and moving him toward a fuller, integrated, spiritual awareness.

Jesus' wish to remain hidden collides with the escalating demands of the world. We all face similar situations when we think we can hide and remain anonymous. We might have thought our concern extends only to those who are most familiar to us—our families, our friends, our inner circle. Jesus' awareness is at this stage of development, and he responds tribally rather than globally.

The nameless woman, a Greek, is an outsider and considered unclean. She comes to Jesus for a clear purpose—the healing of her daughter. She embodies the comprehensive quality of the vast maternal heart. Her story challenges bigotry, self-interest, and any notion her heartrending concerns are not also our own.

When the story is first told in the Gospel of Mark, the point is clear: this forceful and persistent character is an assertive woman who confronts male propriety and creates a disturbance. Like the tenacious, grieving, mythological mother Demeter (who sought the release of her daughter Persephone from the grasp of Hades) this Canaanite woman will not be deterred. She defies cultural norms, and, as an outcast, she throws herself at Jesus' feet pleading for help and healing for her child.

Jesus' response is to ignore her. He plays out the ancient script of domination and patriarchy. The disciples also attempt to dismiss her, but she will not go away. The voice of the mother is the stronger force. She symbolizes the fierce egoless state of care for another typical of the Great Mother archetype. The woman is forcing herself into the conversation and consciousness of the times. She is determined to be heard and for the needs of her child to be addressed. She comes from marginalization and estrangement, emerging with clear purpose beyond ego, and beyond the cultural limitations of borders or gender. Her presence is shot through with the clarity and strength of a mother's love and determination.

Finally, in Jesus' last attempt to deter her, he says he must feed his children, the children of his tribe, before feeding the dogs. This is a harsh reaction to the heartbreaking plea of a mother who is begging for help. Such a response clearly reflects the values of ethnocentric thinking. Jesus' reaction is a mirror reflecting the ways in which we set boundaries as to who is worthy of our care and concern.

The woman replies to the insult in a most astonishing way. She says even the dogs get the crumbs that fall to the floor, indicating she willingly accepts whatever help is available in whatever way it shows up. She has resisted one of the greatest temptations of the human ego. In response to the insult Jesus leveled, she refrains from becoming defensive. The woman understands that when we react defensively in these kinds of situations we always lose. She offers a solution leading to reconciliation and healing. She remains clear and committed to her purpose. She will take whatever serves the need. Just as with Demeter, who persistently pressed Zeus for help, a compromise is proposed and her daughter is returned to her.

The woman's response lifts her up to her rightful place at the table. Something shifts in Jesus. He seems to recognize that he has been caught in old patterns and limiting beliefs. He understands that the reach of the awakened heart will extend to all, regardless of race or gender. The Sacred Feminine brings the inclusive, compassionate heart into a patriarchal and parochial consciousness. Jesus expresses respect for the wisdom of her response to him and pronounces the daughter healed.

Each action of the Canaanite woman is well thought out. Each response is elegant and deliberate. Her method leads to healing and transformation. She perseveres with a clear sense of urgency, determination, and a willingness to push through the limitations others place upon her. She stays centered and focused on her intention. She resists defensiveness and anger. This nameless woman's wisdom allows her responses to be authentic and wise. She creates a way for healing to happen, while also leaving a legacy of broadened awareness.

REFLECTIONS & QUESTIONS

1. There is safety and comfort within the boundaries of our own communities. The downside is we can become too insular.
   How have you experienced the effects of exclusive, tribal thinking? How have you participated in it? Are there times when it is appropriate? If so, how do we maintain boundaries with wisdom and heart?

2. A clear sense of urgency and determination; the willingness to push through cultural and self-imposed limitations; remaining centered, purposeful, without defensiveness or anger; and openness to our inner guidance all contribute to healing and wholeness.
   As you reflect on these qualities, what evidence have you seen of their power in your own life and the lives of others?

Bodhicitta:
The Centurion's Servant

*W*hen *Jesus had entered Capernaum, a centurion*
came to him, asking for help. "Lord," he said, "my
servant lies at home paralyzed, suffering terribly."
Jesus said to him, "Shall I come and heal him?"

The centurion replied, "Lord, I do not deserve to have you
come under my roof. But just say the word, and my servant
will be healed. For I myself am a man under authority, with
soldiers under me. I tell this one, 'Go,' and he goes; and that
one, 'Come,' and he comes. I say to my servant, 'Do this,' and
he does it."

When Jesus heard this, he was amazed and said to those
following him, "Truly I tell you, I have not found anyone in
Israel with such great faith…. Then Jesus said to the centu-
rion, "Go! Let it be done just as you believed it would." And
his servant was healed at that moment.

MATTHEW 8:5-10,13 (NIV)

THIS MAN IS A SOLDIER WHO WORKED HIMSELF UP
through the ranks to become a centurion. He has seen con-
flicts and human casualties. He bears the challenges of main-

taining the authority and leadership for the 100 soldiers in his care. But on this day, things are different. He is deeply troubled by the particular need of one individual—a servant. When Jesus enters Capernaum, the centurion is waiting.

The soldier comes in his full warrior regalia. His helmet—an impressive plume of horsetail—and his leather and metal tunic call attention to his status and role in the community. He comes before the itinerant Jewish mystic, Jesus, with a clear sense of urgency and purpose. His servant, he says, "is paralyzed, suffering terribly."

Stop and consider this scene. Do not move on too quickly. Let the urgency and concern enter and connect you to the shared experience of sentient life. At some time in our lives, we all experience events that paralyze us and cause us deep suffering.

Rather than sending a messenger to command help, as we might expect of a powerful officer, in this version the centurion goes directly to Jesus. Shantideva, the eighth century Buddhist master, said, "Through sorrow, pride is driven out." In the face of another's suffering, and driven by a deep concern for another's welfare, we might find ourselves asking and doing things we would never do for ourselves. When compassion opens the door of the heart, pride vanishes like a vapor. The centurion has come out of hiding behind his role and society's expectations of him to seek help for another. Jesus' answer is less a question than a possibility, "Shall I come and heal him?" The centurion's swift response, "I do not deserve to have you come under my roof….," leaves us to speculate what was at the root of declining such a generous offer.

A centurion's home in those times was elaborate, especially in comparison to the modest homes Jesus often visited. Even with the greatness of his house and his powerful position as a soldier, he does not consider himself worthy of Jesus' visit. The house to which the centurion refers is not merely a physical structure, but an interface between our personal and public worlds. The walls hold our personal identities, our stories and dramas. But even the most beautiful facades contain shadows and secrets. Despite our positions, no matter how dressed up and agreeable our appearances, we often live with feelings of unworthiness and shame. Shame can have a debilitating effect on us when an event triggers fear of what others will think of us. We also experience shame when our behavior violates our personal values. The source of these feelings might stem from an experience in childhood. They become internalized into "basic shame," feeling states that can affect us throughout life in negative and often unconscious ways. Such states can undermine healthy relationships. Like the centurion, we might attempt to conceal our shame by taking positions of authority or dominating others. Some of us hide our shame in notions of being special. The centurion does not want Jesus to see him where he lives. He does not want to risk what others might think of him if Jesus comes to his home. The centurion is not yet ready to be known in such a deeply revealing way. Perhaps the centurion is saying to Jesus, "If you really knew me.... If you really saw what goes on in the private places of my heart and mind, you would see I am someone other than who I appear to be." What goes on in the house of the centurion in terms of discord and in his private affairs, goes on in our own hearts and at our own hearths from time to time.

Regardless of what the centurion's personal issues might be, his primary concern is for the wellbeing of his servant. Lynn McTaggart writes of research from the field of neurobiology that leads many scientists to think there is an intrinsic connection, or what she terms "bond," between all life that prompts us to act compassionately. "Rather than domination, our most basic urge is to reach out to another human being...the urge to empathize, to be compassionate, and to help others altruistically—is not the exception to the rule, but our natural state of being." [60] The centurion stepped out of his sense of being special or different and experienced a deeper connection to his own true, tender heart. He has genuinely responded to the pain of another.

Something unexpected enters the mix when the centurion offers an alternative to Jesus. Rather than coming to his home, he proposes that Jesus do the healing work right where he is. He says that, as an officer, he takes orders and carries them out. He also gives orders and these orders are promptly obeyed. It is not necessary for him to be in the kitchen to know the pot will be stirred. The centurion says to Jesus, "Why don't you just give an order for the servant to be healed?"

Not only does this reveal faith, as Jesus notes, but the centurion also is a bit audacious to be instructing the master. What a curious mix of exchanges and unlikely doings. Jesus, however, is open to the suggestion. He responds as if saying, "Why didn't I think of that before?" It is a little "A-ha!" moment for Jesus. While acknowledging the faith of the centurion, Jesus illustrates his own openness to possibility. This trait, which Jesus reveals in other stories, as well, demonstrates a quality of evolving awareness and ascending consciousness, a quality of higher-level spiritual intelligence indicative of a great teacher.

In the Buddhist tradition, the compassionate recognition of suffering and the desire to attend to it is called *bodhicitta*. One who has bodhicitta as the primary motivation for all of her or his activities is called a *bodhisattva*.[61] The legendary goddess from ancient Buddhism, Tara, symbolizes the nature of a bodhisattva. She has been called the "River of Compassion." She hears the cries and suffering of the world, heals disease, and comforts sentient beings. Her compassionate response is a vow to forego her own liberation and stay on Earth in order to dispense mercy and relieve pain. Compassion is expressed as the feminine principle of the soul residing in both genders. This is symbolically represented by figures that are female, androgynous, or male. The work of bodhicitta is to make a difference in the world through loving kindness. When the feminine aspect of care meets the soul's masculine principle of action, the powerful possibility of wholeness, healing, and compassionate action is born. Jesus, in his healing work and teachings, demonstrates the nature of a bodhisattva by choosing to walk among the suffering rather than retreating from the concerns of the world.

In the centurion's response to his servant's situation, we get a glimpse of his awakening compassionate nature. He is motivated to help, to seek relief for the suffering servant. Even a Roman soldier, who symbolizes a system of oppression, can embody a balance of heartfelt concern and action, the integration of yin and yang, the male and female principles of the divine. In the words of Gautama, the Buddha, "Moments before you develop bodhicitta you can be the most evil being in the whole universe, but the moment after you develop bodhicitta, you instantly become the most noble, kind and precious being in the whole universe." Then he said, "Developing bodhicitta is taking birth in the family of enlightenment."[62]

Faith is an essential ingredient in the healing outcome. In the ancient Aramaic, the word for faith is *haimanuta*, referring to a secure connection to spiritual understanding. Faith is the active participation of individual will, sometimes defined as "firm action." This is not just an intellectual exercise, but it is deeply grounded in compassion, in the heart. The centurion's faith, as demonstrated in action and will, ignites the healing power of the Christ. Christ, the awakened spiritual consciousness embodied in Jesus, is the catalyst that transforms terrible suffering; and, at that instant the servant is healed. This healing does not depend on the healing presence, the physical form of a healer. This is how prayer works. The dynamic that is generated when pure and powerful intention strikes the chord of the divine, resonates as wholeness, as answered prayer, as healing.

REFLECTIONS & QUESTIONS

1. In the face of another's suffering, we might find
   ourselves asking for things we would never ask for
   ourselves.
   *Have you ever had the experience of asking for
   another what you would never ask for yourself?
   Reflect on what this was like for you.*

2. Shame is the feeling that we are inherently wrong or
   flawed. We are unaware of the negative effects this
   basic shame has on our happiness.
   *What would it be like to be more aware of your
   feelings of shame as they arise? Can you imagine
   being gentle and compassionate when feeling shame,
   rather than judging yourself for being inherently
   flawed?*

3. *Bodhicitta* can be translated as "awakening mind" or
   "mind of enlightenment" or referred to as the union
   of compassion and wisdom. The action of bodhicitta
   is to make a loving and positive difference for others.
   *What does compassion mean to you? How do you
   experience compassion? How is it similar to or
   different from sympathy?*

4. Faith is the active participation of individual will,
   sometimes defined as "firm action." This is not just
   an intellectual exercise but rather an exercise that is
   deeply grounded in feeling, in the heart.
   *How do you define faith? How is faith different from
   or similar to belief? What does it mean to you that
   faith is energized by feeling?*

Radiance:
The Transfiguration

After six days Jesus took Peter, James and John with him and led them up a high mountain, where they were all alone. There he was transfigured before them. His clothes became dazzling white, whiter than anyone in the world could bleach them. And there appeared before them Elijah and Moses, who were talking with Jesus. Peter said to Jesus, "Rabbi, it is good for us to be here. Let us put up three shelters—one for you, one for Moses and one for Elijah." Then a cloud appeared and covered them, and a voice came from the cloud: "This is my Son, whom I love. Listen to him!" Suddenly, when they looked around, they no longer saw anyone with them except Jesus.

There he was transfigured before them. His face shone like the sun, and his clothes became as white as the light.

MATTHEW 17:2 (NIV)

As he was praying, the appearance of his face changed, and his clothes became as bright as a flash of lightning.... Peter and his companions were very sleepy, but when they became fully awake, they saw his glory and the two men standing with him. As the men were leaving Jesus, Peter said to him, "Master, it is good for us to be here. Let us put up

three shelters—one for you, one for Moses and one for Elijah."
(He did not know what he was saying).

LUKE 9:29, 32-33 (NIV)

＊＊＊

HERE IS A PATH WORN BY OTHERS WHO HAVE GONE
before, winding its way among the boulders, narrowing in
the overgrowth of low-growing shrubs. The travelers along
this path ascend. Their sandals scrape against the rocks.
Leaning forward this way and then shifting again to keep
centered and balanced, they turn into the spiraling rise and
move up, higher and higher. This time, Jesus takes these
others with him: Peter, James, and John.

The Gospel of Mark reads he "…led them up a high
mountain…." To lead is purposeful. It is also careful. At
times, Jesus glances back to see how they are doing. When
he comes to gnarled roots splayed across the path, he
stops, signaling caution or extending a steady hand. On
the smooth, twisting parts, he glides on before them. For a
moment he is out of sight. Then they turn a corner and see
him moving on ahead. Finally they reach the mountaintop.

There is clarity is such high places. One can look out in
all directions. The varied colors and textures of the earth are
spread out below them. Animals and humans appear small.
Their movements are barely discernible. The sun illuminates
the landscape, creating shadows as the earth rotates. The
only sound is the breeze whistling around the corners. The
air has a slightly sweet, sacramental taste as the men take in
deep gulps to catch their breath. At the top of the mountain
there is a different viewpoint, an elevated awareness. This

Ruth Ann Lonardelli

is a holy place of divine revelation. From this perspective, there are no separate factions. There is a sweeping landscape, which is diverse and yet also connected. Many paths wind around the mountain's base. There are many approaches. Moving up the trail, all the paths merge at the top and become one. Sacred Oneness is the prevailing perspective in consciousness.

This story appears in all of the synoptic gospels, although the details differ in each text. Mark, the oldest version, tells us that Jesus "…was transfigured before them. His clothes became dazzling white, whiter than anyone in the world could bleach them." In Matthew, "There he was transfigured before them. His face shone like the sun, and his clothes became as white as the light." And in Luke, "As he was praying, the appearance of his face changed, and his clothes became as bright as a flash of lightning…."

In one version, the disciples, despite the dazzling radiance all around them, slip into a state of drowsiness. They do not understand Jesus' spiritual teaching. They are asleep to the deeper meaning; they are still in the process of awakening. The disciples are jolted awake by the apparition of the ancient prophets Moses and Elijah, who suddenly show up. These two figures come from the ancient Hebrew lineage of prophets and law. They are a reminder of our religious ancestors. Jesus will teach a spiritual way that differs from those who preceded him. He is also wise enough to know and respect that we are all standing on the ground cultivated by others who have gone before us.

Peter is historically recognized as the founder of the Christian church, but he does not fully comprehend the new spiritual consciousness in the Jesus teachings. He reveals the limitations of his understanding when he says to Jesus, "Master, it is good for us to be here. Let us put up three shelters (tents) one for you, one for Moses, and one for Elijah. (He did not know what he was saying.)" Peter's vision is still limited to material awareness and spotlight consciousness. He is unable to see beyond the boundaries of his perspective. He is focused on old ways of doing things. Peter wants to do the right thing, and he believes he is doing so by creating structures in which the divine can be protected and contained. It is easy to sympathize with Peter at this point. We are half-awake to spiritual understanding, and we often want to do something to contain and protect sacred revelations, only to find they are not to be caught in the old familiar ways. They belong to another reality. These insights are ineffable and defy our attempts to control and hold onto them by conventional means.

Then a large cloud appears and surrounds them. The disciples tremble in fear as the cloud overcomes them and a celestial voice booms forth, saying, "Listen to him." In this way, the message of Jesus and his vision of Sacred Oneness are affirmed.

The writers of Matthew and Luke borrowed heavily from the stories of the earlier Gospel of Mark, and they also included their own distinctive touches. Some of these touches were intended to place the events within the tradition of prophecy. Others were meant to teach us something about the authors' knowledge of the spiritual meaning in the narratives. Although all of the gospels weave interpretations from their individual and cultural perspective, the culture of those times was remarkably diverse and not purely Judaic. Greco-Roman stories of sun-drenched, radiant gods and goddess on mountaintops were familiar motifs to the people of the times. Stories such as these would have indicated divine revelation. From the *Hymn to Demeter*, written in the sixth century B.C.E.:

> From the divine body of the goddess a light shone afar, while golden tresses spread down over her shoulders, so that the strong house was filled with brightness as with lightning.[63]

Discussions about the mythical or theological references of these stories are interesting, but they can also be a distraction from the deep spiritual significance they convey. At its essence, the story of transfiguration transcends both theology and tradition.

Progression through ascension of consciousness brings Jesus to the heights of spiritual realization. This is a circuitous path that culminates in a sublime manifestation of enlightenment. At the sacred mountaintop of awareness, Jesus arrives at the intersection bridging heaven and Earth. He meets and acknowledges the wisdom and gifts of his ancestors. He rises up to receive heaven descending, and the merger of these two aspects results in radiance incarnate. The physical form of the master is imbued with transcendental glory: "His face shone like the sun." Jesus reveals the brilliance of floodlight consciousness offering an expanded and inclusive view of creation. There is no separation here, but a perfect blending of heaven and Earth, of transcendent and immanent, in sacred union. If Jesus was tempted to ascend even higher and leave earthly suffering behind him, we do not know. As the Christ, the Bodhisattva, he descends the mountain to face the suffering before him. But now he can move through the challenges ahead of him, from the healing of a demonic child to his own resurrection experience. The radiance of enlightenment has left him saturated in spirit and clear about what is his to do.

REFLECTIONS & QUESTIONS

1. There is clarity in high places of inspiration. We can rest and gain a perspective that assists us when we return to our everyday lives.
   Where do you go for rest and inspiration? What do you receive in these places that helps you?

2. We can experience moments of pure illumination that transcend the limits of theology, and traditions in which we feel the radiance of essential sacred being.
   Have you experienced such moments? If so, what was your experience? If not, how might you imagine such moments to be?

3. Jesus is wise enough to know and respect his religious heritage. He is also moving in a new spiritual direction.
   How do you regard the religious values and training you received in the past? Have you made peace with the things you were taught and which you no longer believe? What values from your religious past are still meaningful for you?

4. When transcendent moments are realized within the context of our everyday lives, we experience a fuller sense of the sacred. This is where the transcendent and immanent qualities intersect.
   What is your understanding of how the transcendent and immanent are realized and how they are one?

The Second Spring:
Arise Daughter, Your Faith
Has Made You Whole

When Jesus had again crossed over by boat to the other side of the lake, a large crowd gathered around him while he was by the lake. Then one of the synagogue leaders, named Jairus, came, and when he saw Jesus, he fell at his feet. He pleaded earnestly with him, "My little daughter is dying. Please come and put your hands on her so that she will be healed and live." So Jesus went with him.

A large crowd followed and pressed around him. And a woman was there who had been subject to bleeding for twelve years. She had suffered a great deal under the care of many doctors and had spent all that she had, yet instead of getting better, she grew worse. When she heard about Jesus, she came up behind him in the crowd and touched his cloak, because she thought, "If I just touch his clothes, I will be healed." Immediately her bleeding stopped; and she felt in her body that she was freed from her suffering. At once Jesus realized that power had gone forth from him. He turned around in the crowd and said, "Who touched my clothes?" "You see the people crowding against you," his disciples answered, and yet you can ask, 'Who touched me?'" But Jesus kept looking around to see who had done it. Then the woman, knowing what had happened to her, came and fell at his feet and, trembling with fear, told him the whole truth. He said to her, "Daughter, your faith has healed you. Go in peace, and be freed from your suffering."

While Jesus was still speaking, some people came from the house of Jairus, the synagogue leader. "Your daughter is dead," they said. "Why bother the teacher anymore?" Overhearing what they said, Jesus told him, "Don't be afraid; just believe." He did not let anyone follow him except Peter, James, and John, the brother of James. When they came to the home of the synagogue leader, he saw a commotion, with people crying and wailing loudly. He went in and said to them, "Why all this commotion and wailing? The child is not dead but asleep." But they laughed at him.

After he put them all out, he took the child's father and mother and the disciples who were with him, and went in where the child was. He took her by the hand and said to her, "Talitha koum," which means, "Little girl, I say to you, get up!" Immediately the girl got up and began to walk about (she was twelve years old). At this they were completely astonished. He gave strict orders not to let anyone know about this, and told them to give her something to eat.

MARK 5:21-43 (NIV)

IMAGINE BEING ONE OF THEM, STRAINING TO HEAR WHAT is happening, moving with the others toward the action. At first, there is the usual murmuring, the shuffling associated with a group of people gathering together. Then you can feel the energy of the crowd change as the woman approaches.

She is running. The look on her face is intense, focused. She runs as if she is being pursued, but no one appears to be running after her. The crowd parts as she approaches. Not to clear the way, but to stand separate from her. She is unclean, untouchable, a woman who has been suffering from hemorrhages for twelve years. Menstruation, a deeply ingrained taboo in this culture, evokes fear, disgust, and shame. She doesn't acknowledge the others. She is intent and clear. She is looking for Jesus. She heard he would be here today. She pushes on through the crowd. The crowd is so large now it is impossible to avoid touching her. People recoil in disgust. They mutter and gesture as if to brush away any contact with her. She is among us. She is also one of us. We catch just a few words as she pushes past, "If only…." she says, her eyes focused, her brow wrinkled, as she presses on toward the person at the center of the gathering crowd.

She is the embodiment of Everywoman. She is bearing the history of every woman's experience. She is carrying a burden of shame. This nameless one is an outcast, unacceptable, undervalued. She is not good enough. This is the woman who has endured terrible rituals of purification to prove her worth and readiness. She is sacrificed on the funeral pyre of her husband. She has been burned at the stake for practicing her craft. She has been oppressed and suppressed until, *on this day*, something takes hold of her, and she rises up and runs with strength she did not realize she possessed. She runs on, in spite of the collective messages and thoughts crowding her mind: You can't do this! Who do you think you are? You are not good enough. You are not worthy. She runs through the multitude of voices. She knows that if she keeps going and pushes through the barriers of culture—including the opinions others hold of her and her own limited, self-deprecating thoughts and beliefs—she can touch that which is holy and she will become whole. She will shed the past and move on into a new life.

She has pushed her way in, and now she can see Jesus through the pressing crowd. He is directly before her. He is making his way slowly. Those traveling with him urge Jesus to move along quickly. There is an emergency up ahead. A young girl is gravely ill. He must hurry to save her. We hear these heartbreaking words from the child's father, *"My little daughter is at the point of death. Come and lay your hands on her, so that she may be made well* (Greek: *sothe*—healed or saved), *and live."* Jesus is reassuring the father that his daughter will be healed. Such assurances at a time like this! Such audacious calmness!

Then, the woman is right behind him. She thinks she can discreetly touch his robe and her touch will go unnoticed. She thinks she can reach through the chaos of need and desperation and touch him, and then she will be made well. She reaches out, carefully, so her gesture remains unseen. What she is doing is radical, even dangerous. She is an outrageous sight. She is an unclean woman, on par with a leper or outcast. She dares to touch a rabbi! "Just a touch—just one slight touch of his garment…." Her fingers, soiled, discolored, and etched with years of hard work, reach out.

He stops and turns. "Who touched me?" he asks. His friends laugh. "Who hasn't touched you? Look at all these people. It could have been anyone." Sometimes his questions baffle them. He is not deterred. "This is different," he tells them. The woman is aware of being found out. What she hoped to ask for herself in secret—so as to avoid calling attention to herself so no one would be disturbed, so she would not trouble anyone, so her needs would not make themselves known—is now out in the open. Her will and a determination she hardly recognizes in herself have moved her out of the societal secret of shame, out of the comfort zone of her private pain, and into publicly making her need and condition visible, along with her deepest heartfelt desire. She is standing up for herself and her wholeness. The crowd is at a standstill. She does not know what to expect next. Will he make an example of her, an example of impertinence? Will she once again be the object of humiliation? Her face is hot and flushed. She is afraid, but she has gone so far now and there is no turning back. She answers, "It was I." He turns and greets her. "Arise, daughter. Your faith has made you whole." Immediately her flow ceases.

The story does not end here. This woman comes to experience healing. That was "Act One." There is a trajectory here. She approaches him from behind. What lies ahead is "Act Two." Jesus moves on with his friends and the father of the girl who is ill. As they approach the family home, they see mourners already gathered. They are greeted with the report that the little girl is dead. But the teacher refutes this, "No, she is not dead, she is sleeping." Because she is considered to be dead, she is also unclean. The master goes to her and touches her, saying, "Arise, daughter, you are healed." And the young girl gets up from her deathbed, restored and well.

These two female figures are never named. They are simply called, "daughter." They are not named because they are the collective female experience. These figures also represent the feminine aspect of the divine that has been marginalized, outcast, and believed to be dead. In this story, the limits of society and culture, the limitations of self-talk and self-loathing are overcome, and a rightful place in the family of humanity claimed. When we see these two characters as representative of stages of the archetypal feminine story, rather than as distinct and separate individuals, we see the progression of a woman's life from what no longer serves her to renewal and possibilities. It represents an emptying of everything that drains us.

The adult woman is said to be hemorrhaging for twelve years. It is impossible to hemorrhage for so long. Such a condition would have resulted in death long ago. The young girl is also twelve years old. The traditional meaning associated with the number twelve might point to the twelve tribes of Israel. However, the symbolism of the number twelve predates Judaism. Number twelve represents completion, the circling and cycling movement of the heavenly bodies like the female cycling of menses.

When the cycle comes to completion, this is woman at midlife. The flow of the hemorrhagic woman ceases. She enters a new phase of life. At this juncture, her identity shifts and another female experience emerges. What comes forth is the new self, which was thought to be dead, but as it turns out, is only asleep.

Midlife offers the possibilities for deep change in a woman's life. This is a time to experience profound healing of history and image. Women in their childbearing years are often acutely aware of their biological clock ticking away. Women, prompted by menopause, become aware of another biological clock ticking as we face old age and our mortality. We feel as though we no longer have time for the old dramas and pain of the past. This is when we tell ourselves that if we don't speak up now, there might never be another chance. When we press on, speaking up for our wholeness and healing, we show the way forward, encouraging others to do the same. As we press on past all we have endured, individually and collectively, the seemingly ceaseless flow of life's blood, which ravages all people and all species, stops. We press beyond what is, to what can be. We stand up for ourselves and for healing. In doing so, we stand up for others and for all life.

The Chinese refer to a woman's midlife transition as her "Second Spring." The possibilities exist for a new beginning. In this story, the young girl represents this return to life, a second spring. She who was thought to be dead (in an unclean condition, like the hemorrhagic woman) is now at the springtime of life. A hopeless situation has been healed. From here Jesus gives the command, "Give her something to eat." Like a good Jewish mother, he instructs her family to nurture her, to feed her. Andrew Harvey, philosopher and author, notes, "Images of food and nourishment...have always belonged to the mythology of the Great Mother."[64] This food is essential to life. This is the sustaining physical meal as well as what nourishes our hearts and spirits.

Gospel stories such as this one are heavily imbued with the spirit of the Sacred Feminine. The origins of this story could be from regional women's folklore. Women made significant contributions to the early Christian movement. We know some of their names: Johanna, Junia, Priscilla, Grapte, Thecla, and Susanna, to name a few. Some were educated and wealthy, and many were influential. Some scholars think parts of the New Testament contain accounts written by women. Perhaps this was one of them. The presence of women in these stories is no accident; they reflect the importance women played in the early Jesus movement. In addition to men, women would have made contributions, from their own perspectives, to the process of selecting which stories needed to be told and retained. Their inclusion offers another voice in the male-dominated religious hierarchy. The implications of this are enormous, not only for women but for men, as well. When we understand the Jesus movement as an inclusive teaching, rather than just giving lip service to a transcendent theology, we at last obtain a glimpse of a spirituality in which no person is left out.

In the traditional understanding of this story, Jesus, the healer and miracle worker, was the healing agent for the hemorrhagic woman and the young girl. But in a mystical sense, Jesus acts as the catalyst for healing, the pivotal point of transformation, the portal through which we pass to emerge, restored into new and vibrant life. Here he exemplifies Mother-God through whom new life comes forth. The first daughter touches his garment. Jesus is aware the woman reached out to him for healing; however, he tells her it is *her* faith that made her whole. It is her willingness to push on, to reach out, and to hold on to the vision of her wholeness and push past society's claims on her. She stands up for herself and finds her voice. Although she is trembling, she finally speaks up. "It is I," she says. Her will and determination, and her humility have made her whole. We look to others to heal us, but the best teachers are those who find ways to help us ignite the spark of wholeness within ourselves. They help us remember that what we thought was dead is still very much alive in us. The Jesus of this story is the healer who understands that wholeness exists as a potentiality, activated through will, determination, and risk. This is an ironic departure from the traditional understanding that our faith in Jesus is the way for healing to happen. Jesus remarks that it is the faith of the first woman that has made her whole. The word "faith" is a verb in the original Hebrew. It is something we do with a particular quality that is fundamental to our nature. Faith is activated when we act with passion from our deepest, most authentic selves. Buddhist teacher Sharon Salzberg notes that faith means, "to place the heart upon."[65] This is certainly the faith of the nameless woman. She is determined to make contact with the power of healing. She wholeheartedly pushes through the crowd of limiting beliefs to reach her goal. In this story, Jesus sees the potential of wholeness and life in these two daughters. *He has faith in them!* The hemorrhagic woman is healed. The young girl of this story, Jesus says repeatedly, is not dead—she is only sleeping. Jesus extends his hand, offering support for her to arise. Support is a crucial element in these stories. Support is love in the form of care and concern calling us forth and helping us connect with our sacred potential—what is alive and well within us.

REFLECTIONS & QUESTIONS

1. In a mystical sense, Jesus, as an embodiment of the Christ, acts as the catalyst for healing, the pivotal point of transformation available for all people, the portal through which we pass to emerge, restored into new and vibrant life.
What is the difference between thinking of Jesus as a superhuman God or as an embodiment of compassion, the pivot point, and the portal through which we pass?

2. Midlife offers the potential for real change, an experience of deep, profound healing of history and image.
Reflect on the stages of your life and what the changes in your life mean for you spiritually.

3. Faith is an active, whole-hearted determination to action, and it plays a powerful part in healing.
How is the definition of faith as an active process similar to or different from your own understanding? Do you experience faith as an activity?

The Space In-Between:
Mary and Martha

As Jesus and his disciples were on their way, he came to a village where a woman named Martha opened her home to him. She had a sister called Mary, who sat at the Lord's feet listening to what he said. But Martha was distracted by all the preparations that had to be made. She came to him and asked, "Lord, don't you care that my sister has left me to do the work by myself? Tell her to help me!"

"Martha, Martha," the Lord answered, "you are worried and upset about many things, but few things are needed—or indeed only one. Mary has chosen what is better, and it will not be taken away from her."

LUKE 10: 38-42 (NIV)

IN AN OUTPOURING OF LOVE AND HOSPITALITY, MARTHA opens her home to Jesus and his friends. She steps into action and begins preparations, but then she becomes aware of the overwhelming task before her. No wonder she wants Mary to help her, but Mary is besotted with the love of learning, sitting in rapt attention at the master's feet. Martha challenges Jesus to listen to her need for help and command Mary to assist her. But instead, Jesus rebuffs Martha. He tells Martha she is too worried about worldly details and that Mary has the right idea.

This story is a timeless conundrum for all of us. On the one hand, we get it that Mary is an example for us. She is following her heart, as well as challenging the traditional, limited roles for women. On the other hand, Martha's contribution is being diminished, and she is stuck with all the less glamorous work. Jesus tells her that Mary is making the better choice of learning over labor.

I empathize with Martha, which speaks to how often I have found myself in her position. I also feel envy and admiration for Mary, who is able to withstand the pull of societal expectations and follow her heart's deep calling. Contrast is a compelling story-telling device. When we are presented with what appears as opposites, we are immediately drawn to make comparisons, to ferret out illuminating distinctions or make a choice between the two. At a deeper level, contrast works to reveal the lesson lying in the space between the two opposing positions.

I recognize both Mary and Martha as parts of my own internal conflict, and in talking with others I realize I am not alone. Just when I get settled into my Mary mind, tending to what I long to do, my Martha thoughts show up waving a to-do list a mile long. She is "worried and distracted by many things." She can endlessly "what if." She wants everything to be done on time, and sometimes it is difficult to enlist others in her vision. Partners and family members have other priorities. It is easy for my inner Martha to change a few letters in my name and turn me into a resentful and angry "Martyr."

Martha makes harsh demands on herself and experiences an intensely painful sense of being separate and alone in her need for recognition and support. Such a sense of aloneness might arise from a core belief of being somewhat different from others in a negative way, of being inherently flawed and unworthy of loving care. Martha, like many of us, attempts to manage this feeling of being separate from others by striving for perfection or engaging in the similarly self-defeating practice of over-care. Neither of these approaches can ameliorate the suffering. The only antidote to this misery is self-acceptance, gentleness with our humanness, and cultivation of our expanding, awakening heart. Then we will realize that the richness of our human experience lies not just in doing, but also in being. If I understand what Jesus is actually saying to Martha, I hear something I have longed to hear all my life: *You don't have to earn this love.* When Jesus rebuffs Martha, he is also calling our inner critics out to answer for all the ways we have been held hostage to the expectations we have placed on ourselves.

We all want a chance to develop our gifts and expand our learning, and there is Mary—she is doing it! However, my inner Mary has challenges too. Do not think she does not know what Martha wants and needs. Do not assume she hasn't weighed the cost of following her dreams. She knows what others might think of her—steeping in the pleasure of spiritual learning while her sister, Martha, is in the kitchen. It takes commitment and courage to stay the course and not succumb to the demand of these pressures. It takes courage to be gentle with ourselves. We need to become strong enough to risk the disapproval of others in order to realize our true calling. When we do so, we are shredding our addiction to judging ourselves. We also lose our fierce hold on judging others as well. When I was growing up, a maniacal "Martha" ran our household. Any interest in reading, writing, and studying always was at odds with more tangible, productive chores. As an out-of-control Martha, we create a strict and stifling atmosphere. But as a wise and warm Martha, we can create a warm, welcoming environment that balances doing with being.

There are times when we need to have a conversation with our inner Martha. There are times when we need to relinquish our grip on details and follow our Mary hearts. We also need to be willing to step up for each other, cover the details, and be a Martha for our friends and partners. This balanced approach allows us all the time and energy we need to pursue our callings. The obvious answer to this dilemma is that, in the best of all partnership worlds, the tasks of life are shared in a state of mutual support. I like to think this is what happened for Martha in this Jesus story. If it was anything like what I have experienced in spiritual communities, helpers show up from the most unexpected places and somehow the work gets done.

We need both the Mary and Martha aspects of ourselves. When Mary and Martha come into balance, when we release our hold on perfection and follow our heart's deep calling, we come into a fuller experience of a more harmonious life and a greater sense of spiritual fulfillment.

REFLECTIONS & QUESTIONS

1. Sometimes our willingness and desire to serve far exceeds our internal reserves. We become stressed when we place unrealistic expectations on ourselves. *How have you managed this kind of situation in your own life? How do you resist the temptation to become resentful of others who are not motivated to help out?*

2. Are we born innately lovable? Do we have to earn love?
   What does this mean to you? Do you feel that love must be earned, or do you feel innately lovable? Why? Why not?

3. Martha suffers from a sense of feeling separate from others. Her striving for perfection and tendency to over-care is an attempt to soothe her pain. Neither of these approaches can ameliorate the suffering of feeling separate. The only antidote is self-acceptance and gentleness.
   How can you relate to Martha's drive for perfection? What has been your experience with this and with over-care? What does being gentle with yourself mean to you?

4. We can respond to the Mary and Martha parts of ourselves by understanding how to serve ourselves, as well as others.
   How and when have you successfully managed this kind of balance in your life?

Ruth Ann Lonardelli

Bhakti: The Embodiment of the Awakened Heart

W hen one of the Pharisees invited Jesus to have dinner with him, he went to the Pharisee's house and reclined at the table. A woman in that town who lived a sinful life learned that Jesus was eating at the Pharisee's house, so she came there with an alabaster jar of perfume. As she stood behind him at his feet weeping, she began to wet his feet with her tears. Then she wiped them with her hair, kissed them and poured perfume on them.

When the Pharisee who had invited him saw this, he said to himself, "If this man were a prophet, he would know who is touching him and what kind of woman she is—that she is a sinner." ... Then he [Jesus] turned toward the woman and said to Simon, "Do you see this woman? I came into your house. You did not give me any water for my feet, but she wet my feet with her tears and wiped them with her hair. You did not give me a kiss, but this woman, from the time I entered, has not stopped kissing my feet. You did not put oil on my head, but she has poured perfume on my feet. Therefore, I tell you, her many sins have been forgiven—as her great love has shown. But whoever has been forgiven little loves little."

LUKE 7:36-39, 44-47 (NIV)

IN HINDUISM, *BHAKTI* REFERS TO A HEART-CENTERED form of worship based on love and devotion to the Supreme Sacred One. Like the "Beloved" of the Sufis, on the bhakti path expressions of personal love represent the relationship with the divine. Mystical exuberance rather than intellectual musing is the way of bhakti. Bhakti became the religion of the masses of India, just as Sufism appealed to the poor in Islam. Both Bhakti and Sufism are like golden threads connecting us all directly to Sacred Unity, Oneness, and all-encompassing love.

Devotion in the Hindu religion of India requires every bit of the human heart. Devotional practice is a pure, sacred expression of all aspects of our authentic, emotional life. Dancing, gestures (mudras), chanting, and music become the embodied outpouring of the soul's longing for the divine and celebration of divine love. Rather than being instructed in theology, laws, dogma, or doctrine, in devotional worship the only direction is "surrender" of the ego and letting go of the eternal grasping for religious knowledge. In this way, when the mind is clear and the heart fully opened to the essential, primal yearning for God, then there is room for the Beloved to enter and hold the lover in the intoxicating grip of divine love. Everything we have held in reserve—what we have withheld for the sake of appearances—is relinquished. *"Let the lover be disgraceful, crazy, absentminded," says Rumi. "Someone sober will worry about things going badly. Let the lover be."*[66]

Consistent with the androcentric bias against women in religious tradition, it has been supposed the unnamed woman in this scene from the Gospel of Luke had a dubious reputation. In the other gospels where a similar story is told, she is referred to as a prostitute. However, it is highly unlikely a prostitute would be welcomed in the home of a Pharisee or allowed to perform an anointing ritual. Others have speculated that an intimate relationship existed between Jesus and the woman. It was the custom for wives to wash the feet of their husbands. For a woman to let down her hair and use it to dry a man's feet would be considered an act of intimacy. Some others are of the opinion this story is just another example of female subservience to male domination.

Foot washing was an ancient, common practice in Jewish homes. This was an act of hospitality generally offered to guests by women and slaves. The washing of feet also played the role of purification in ritual observances. Later, Christian tradition incorporated foot washing into a ritual associated with humility and service. If we look at this passage from a mystic's awareness, another possibility exists. These verses from Luke, when read as the mystical poetry of the awakened heart, open us to a meaning that transcends other more traditional interpretations. This woman represents the nameless longing for the sacred bridging the separation of society's constructs, roles, and expectations. In this light, she is an impassioned devotee of the divine, a lover of God. The theme of this story is best expressed by the Sufi poet Hafiz, who wrote, "The subject tonight is Love. And, for tomorrow night, as well. As a matter of fact I know of no better topic for us to discuss until we all die!"[67]

This kind of love is expressed by tender acts of surrender and fervent gestures of giving and ecstasy. The woman does not speak. She asks for nothing. She weeps her words and enacts her adoration. When the heart breaks open, deep sorrow at the delusional trance of separation spills out. A kind of bittersweet and intense feeling often accompanies the recognition of the sacred. We approach and honor the divine with the best we have to give. This is an outrageously intimate connection. Some tenderness deep within us arises, bursting forth from the limitation of our roles and personae, to be expressed in the outpouring of our hearts.

Like most of us, the weeping woman comes both with baggage and with gifts of great value. Her past is of no consequence to Jesus. He welcomes her with heartfelt acceptance. The Sufi mystic Rumi addresses this unqualified acceptance, "It doesn't matter if you have broken your vows a thousand times. Still come, yet again come."[68]

The Egyptian divine mother goddess, Bast, was depicted as the lioness, the protector. Her image adorned lavish alabaster jars in which Egyptians stored their perfume. Her ointments were believed to provide protection, and they were often used in funerary rites. Over many generations, Bast was part of Greek and Roman culture. Representations of this goddess and her relevance were commonly known in the region where Jesus lived and traveled. Her appearance as the unnamed woman bearing an alabaster jar of precious oil indicates these stories were still being recited and held meaning during the time of Jesus. The wholehearted acceptance of the Sacred Feminine by Jesus signifies she is welcomed, esteemed, and cherished. While many have intimated the woman is a prostitute, others diminish her by concluding she is a pawn in a patriarchal paradigm. Her tears flow from the deep pain of rejection, the historic trivialization of millions of women, and the suffering she and the beloved are yet to endure. Her tears also flow out of the ocean of love from which she comes. "Our loving," says Rumi, "is the way God's secret gets told." The loving heart of the divine is expressed through her in this intimate gesture.

In contrast to this remarkable scene of the woman's devotion, Simon, the Pharisee, has a lot of questions. He is trying to understand with the limited comprehension of his intellect. Simon is focused in his mental mind. Although Jesus is responding to Simon's comments, he is turned toward the woman—he has turned toward love— directly facing and supporting her when he answers. Jesus is teaching by example, drawing Simon's attention to her enactment of loving devotion and the contrast to Simon's own contracted heart. The woman is washing Jesus' feet with her tears, wiping them with her hair, and anointing him with precious, fragrant oil. She is attending to what is above and below. She has come bearing the gifts of a full heart. She has come as the Sacred Feminine, the heart path of devotion.

This woman, who does not speak, takes action. In the end, there is little we can say about love. This path is lived through care, service, and devotion. A similar practice is observed in Buddhism. Here, washing the feet of enlightened beings represents the cleansing of karma, the clearing of our own misunderstandings and cleansing of our minds.

Jesus explains to Simon that this act of devotion is also about forgiveness. The attention might appear to be focused on the women's personal past, but the implications are much broader. This scene suggests that her ritual of devotion encompasses us all. She brings us here to enact absolution and cleansing from bitterness and resentment. She is free from the oppression of the past. This is the open field of

Loving Spirit that lies beyond our ideas, judgments, and opinions about others and ourselves. The cycles of retribution are ended. In the mystical expansion of pure love, our minds are cleared and our hearts opened.

REFLECTIONS & QUESTIONS

1. The only direction is "surrender" of the ego, letting go of the eternal grasping for religious knowledge. *What is your experience of this kind of letting go?*

2. Mystical exuberance, rather than intellectual musing, is the way of bhakti.
   Are there times in your life when you are like the woman in this story? When are you like Simon, the Pharisee? What are your experiences with each, the gifts and drawbacks?
   Take some time to look up poetry by Rumi and Hafiz.

The Fever:
Simon's Mother-In-Law

W hen Jesus came into Peter's [Simon's] house, he saw Peter's mother-in-law lying in bed with a fever. He touched her hand and the fever left her, and she got up and began to wait on him.

MATTHEW 8:14 (NIV)

Jesus left the synagogue and went to the home of Simon. Now Simon's mother-in-law was suffering from a high fever, and they asked Jesus to help her. So he bent over her and rebuked the fever, and it left her. She got up at once and began to wait on them.

LUKE 4:38-39 (NIV)

As soon as they left the synagogue, they went with James and John to the home of Simon and Andrew. Simon's mother-in-law was in bed with a fever, and they immediately told Jesus about her. So he went to her, took her hand and helped her up. The fever left her and she began to wait on them.

MARK 1:29-31 (NIV)

SHE DOES NOT KNOW HOW LONG SHE HAS BEEN LYING on her bed, but it seems like an eternity. She hears voices from other parts of the house. She thinks she recognizes her daughter's voice, although, at times, it trails off and merges with sounds she cannot identify. Sometimes the voices seem close and she can clearly make out the words. At other times, they sound muffled, far away, distant, as if they are coming from somewhere across the water. A deep weariness overtakes her and she slips in and out of wakefulness. The heat becomes unbearable. She manages to get free from the tangle of blankets, although she has just begged her daughter to heap them around her. She tosses them off, only to find she is shivering from the cold. Her face is colorless and damp. Her whole body is sticky with sweat. She is irritable. She forcefully pushes away offers of food and water. The woman becomes limp, crumbling into a stupor. She is gravely ill and in danger.

After leaving the synagogue, Jesus goes to Simon's house with the others. He arrives to find the household troubled with concern for Simon's mother-in-law. Jesus tends to the situation straight on. In one version, he touches her. In another, he takes her hand and lifts her up. In still another, Jesus bends over her, moving closer to her pain. He offers his care and attention. He stands as a witness to her suffering. She is seen in her worst state through the eyes of love. This empathic connection between the witness and the woman who is suffering transforms her condition. Immediately, she arises from her sick bed. She is energized, restored, and clear about what she is to do. Right away she begins to serve. In this context, her service reflects the work of ministry. The nameless mother-in-law accepts her appointment without hesitation. She steps into her calling as one of Jesus' followers and as someone who lives the transformed life. Her role expands from mother-in-law to being one of the first to be called into ministry.

Simon's unnamed mother-in-law had been in the grip of a high fever. It is interesting that symbolically fever represents anger. Generations of women know the intensity of this condition. Her disease is the anger that sometimes seems to be a blazing fire—an anger that is nameless, as is the mother in this story. This rage is kindled by generations of oppression, suppression, and abuse. It can be fanned into a roar by just one word, one look. A long fuse stretching back into personal and collective history threatens to ignite. Our angry emotions make us feel crazy, and we have been told many times that we are. Just as this fever has been burning for centuries, the bellows feeding the flames have been blowing for generations, too. Her story is our story.

Once we get in touch with this feverish condition, our feelings seem dangerous—even deadly. Unlike the prideful outburst of Herodias, who, when enraged, took revenge by demanding the head of John the Baptist, this kind of anger smolders over time and after countless injustices. The danger here is that the fever will turn against us—as in this story of the nameless mother-in-law—and we will be consumed and destroyed by it. When our dreams and goals seem beyond our reach, and we are unable to take our place as a respected member of the human family; when we hold, at best, a secondary position waiting for changes in the consciousness of our times, despair sets in and anger becomes internalized. We suffer from what the poet Langston Hughes called the "dream deferred":

What happens to a dream deferred?
Does it dry up like a raisin in the sun?
Or fester like a sore—
And then run?
Does it stink like rotten meat?
Or crust and sugar over—
like a syrupy sweet?
Maybe it just sags like a heavy load.
Or does it explode?[69]

A fever need not kill us. In fact, fever is a natural healing response to infection. It is the body's attempt to heal us by making our system aware an invasion has taken place. Something alien has entered us, and a feverish response indicates the immune system is working to overcome the assault. Healthy anger works this way, too. It can empower us out of depression. If we do not face our anger and uncover it's meaning, or we fail to respect our anger as a warning and listen to how we feel, we can become even more powerless. Anger communicates that a violation has occurred, and it is hurtful, damaging, and potentially destructive in a way we can no longer deny.

Often we overlook little stories like these in favor of the more dramatic and colorful ones. However, the story of Simon's nameless mother-in-law is a spiritual jewel. The miracle here is in the empathy and connection with loving-kindness, with the bodhisattva, she who hears the cries of the world. When the nameless woman is seen, we are seen. When she is acknowledged, our pain and our frustration are also acknowledged. "Empathic understanding," writes Marshall Rosenberg, founder of Nonviolent Communication, "is an understanding of the heart in which we see the beauty in the other person, the divine energy in the other…. The goal isn't intellectually understanding it, the goal is emphatically connecting…. It doesn't mean we have to have the same feelings; it means we are *with* the other person. This quality of understanding requires one of the most precious gifts one can give to another: our presence in the moment."[70] From this deep empathy of the heart, a profound connection with the sacred arises in others and in us, and healing happens. To be seen, heard, and acknowledged is the healing our hearts desire.

The fever breaks. Anger has been alchemized into action, and we arise with the nameless woman. We can serve now. Our service could be in the kitchen making matzo. We might be serving elsewhere. Wherever or however we do our work in the world, we go forward knowing more of our sacred connection as a respected member of our community.

REFLECTIONS & QUESTIONS

1. Anger is one of our most challenging human emotions; however, anger often communicates that a violation has occurred. This is hurtful and it requires attention.
   How have you experienced anger in a way that has actually helped you make a positive change in your life? How did the discomfort of anger transform into healing and positive action?

2. The power of simply acknowledging and listening is a profound act of empathy and compassion that offers healing.
   In what ways do you listen with an open heart? What comes up for you in your mind and body when you are listening? Is there resistance, or can you stay with your feelings and listen deeply?
   Have you personally experienced a time when being acknowledged and heard helped you deal with your own anger?

Spontaneous Compassion:
The Widow's Son

*J*esus went to a town called Nain, and his disciples and a
large crowd went along with him. As he approached the
town gate, a dead person was being carried out—the only
son of his mother, and she was a widow. And a large crowd
from the town was with her. When the Lord saw her, his heart
went out to her and he said, "Don't cry." Then he went up and
touched the bier they were carrying him on and the bearers
stood still. He said, "Young man, I say to you, get up!" The
dead man sat up and began to talk, and Jesus gave him back
to his mother. They were all filled with awe and praised God.

LUKE 7:11-16 (NIV)

A SMALL GROUP GATHERS IN THE FIRST LIGHT OF MORN-
ing. Many stories have been circulating about the miracle
worker. Everyone is curious to see what the day will bring.
Women—housewives and grandmothers—come out from
their little cottages to speak with those who are waiting.
Husbands pull on their tunics and follow the women. Children wipe the sleep from their eyes and stand in the doorways to watch what is going on. Soon he appears with the

women and men who travel with him. They are heading out of Capernaum toward a village called "Nain." Peasants and laborers, young and old, join together. They are a procession of townspeople following a dusty path worn by generations of plodding donkeys and meandering sheep and goats. Along the way, farmers leave their fields and join in. As the morning sun spills out across the fields and into the corners and crevices of village life, the group is fully energized. Some are singing, others dancing. A few jostle for a place next to the master. Those who cannot quite keep up with the pace slip to the rear. At first, everyone leans in to hear what is being said up front, but after a while they tire of straining their attention and turn to each other instead. They share their stories and family gossip. Children make up games with stones, and they need to be reined in when things become a little too rowdy. Village dogs wrestle and run in and out of the crowds. At times the crowd stops and sits together at the side of the road. The travelers share their food and wine. Then they resume their journey. A few of them wonder what they are doing wandering farther away from their homes. Some are hopeful, expectant; others are skeptical or just curious; some are grateful for the distraction from their tedious lives. This is a joyful entourage of ragtag villagers who have been swept up in the spirit of what seems life-affirming and full of hope.

As the day is coming to an end, they reach the village of Nain. It is a small, rural town situated in the foothills with views of the surrounding mountains. Nain translates as "beauty," "pleasant," or "green pastures"—all contrasting descriptions to the harsh reality of this place. This village is a sparse little spot inhabited by the very poor.

From the center of Nain, a group of mourners has formed a funeral procession heading out of town. Shrill lamentations and cries of grief echo out over the valley. The mourners reach the gate of the village at the same time as the incoming procession led by Jesus. The two groups stop. They are facing each other. A murmur ripples through the group following Jesus. Their revelry ceases and the mood turns somber. A widow leads the mourners. Her only son is dead. His body is being carried on a bier for burial in the caves outside the village.

Jesus encounters the grieving mother. His expansive compassionate heart goes out to be with her in her sadness. He moves toward the woman. He knows the loss of a loved one is difficult enough, and he recognizes that for a widow to lose her only son is particularly dire. Women have few rights and widows are especially vulnerable. Without a male relative to help her, she is destined for a life of even more poverty and despair. His words and actions are precise and to the point. To the widow, he offers comfort. To the dead son, he commands, "Young man, I order you to get up!" Then Jesus, the Rabbi, touches the bier, which is a radical act in violation of Jewish cleanliness laws. "Immediately, the young man got up and began to speak." Jesus is not responding to any request or prayers or petitions for a miracle. Restoration comes from empathy, compassion, stepping outside the rules of tradition, and clear command.

This is one of the miracle stories portraying Jesus as the great exception. In these kinds of stories, he is capable of healing the sick and resurrecting the dead. Such stories have inspired and frustrated generations of listeners. They are inspiring because they speak to wondrous healing powers that defy death. They are also frustrating because history is heaped high with grieving mothers, impoverished widows for whom no such miracle occurs. There is peril in reading literal and miraculous meaning into this story. When we do so, we limit our understanding of the story as proof of Jesus' superhuman power. So much emphasis is placed on making a case for this kind of Jesus that we have missed important spiritual insight. The miracle stories serve to inspire us—yes, this is true. They do remind us of possibilities, both physical and spiritual. They also work on other levels, allowing us to move up in awareness and down into the depth of our faith.

In this story, two processions, each on quite a different trajectory, meet at the gate of the town. One procession represents hope; the other despair. At the entrance to the village, the two parties come together. Historians and archeologists claim it is unlikely that a gate ever existed at Nain. The tiny village had no walls or fortifications warranting a gate. Gates, thresholds, and doorways represent portals into new worlds. The gate is recognized as, "…a primordial symbol of the Great Mother," a passageway into life. "The feminine principle of the gate is always connected with rebirth…."[71] This gateway is a sacred juncture where life is brought forth. In ancient times, healing rituals re-acting renewal and re-entry into life were commonly performed around gateways.

The themes of rebirth and restoration are at the heart of the Jesus miracles; they are ancient, enduring themes inspired by the cycles in nature, the resurgence of new life after brooding winters or devastating droughts. These themes, which predominate among cultures honoring the feminine face of the sacred, are irrepressible and deeply woven into our human psyches. They offer us hope.

At the gate of "beauty," Nain, Jesus responds to the grieving widow with spontaneous compassion rising up from the depths of his profound recognition of our shared suffering. A miracle is not solicited in any way. "Spontaneous compassion is similar to the feeling a mother has for her one darling child," says fourteenth century Buddhist teacher, Tsong-kha-pa. "She loves that child from the depths of her heart. Whenever that child is in pain or a difficult situation, she fervently wants him or her to pull through."[72] Mercy exists as a natural outpouring of the Immanent Heart of God.

We are all happy for the widow and her son. We are delighted they get another chance. The son receives a reprieve and is restored to life. He will marry and have a family. He will work the fields and help his aging mother. He will grow into a respected elder in his community. His mother will receive the help she needs and enjoy a fulfilling old age surrounded by grandchildren. How does such a story touch us now and heal our own grief in the face of loss? A miracle worker might not arrive to offer a physical healing for our loved one.

Compassion alone cannot heal, but it acts as a healing balm that soothes us, smoothing over the rough spots until we can move forward. Rather than the great exception, Jesus represents the great example informing our hearts and actions. Perhaps not everyone is raised up and made well, but the way we love each other during these tragedies is the miracle. The compassion of Jesus and his willingness to make contact with the afflicted, and his unwavering belief in the resilience of life, give us courage and hope for the trials we will inevitably face. The command is to "get up." This instruction is the heart of the teaching. This is the powerful story of recovery, resilience, and the ability to return to a state of wholeness after being tested by adversity.

REFLECTIONS & QUESTIONS

1. There are several factors leading to recovery in this story. They are:

   - Empathy
   - Compassion
   - Clear expectation, communicated with authority
   - The willingness to step outside the rules and limits of traditional methods, and
   - The unwavering belief in the resilience of life.

   As you reflect on each of these recovery factors, when have you experienced their healing power and potential at work in your own life?

2. An unwavering belief in the resilience of life gives us courage and hope for the trials we will inevitably face. It can be difficult to remember this when we are in the middle of a crisis. At these times, it is especially important to be with others who share and affirm this belief with us.

   How have you supported others in difficult times or been the recipient of support? What has this meant to you?

Ingratitude:
The Pool at Bethesda

One who was there had been an invalid for thirty-eight years. When Jesus saw him lying there and learned that he had been in this condition for a long time, he asked him, "Do you want to get well?"

"Sir," the invalid replied, "I have no one to help me into the pool when the water is stirred. While I am trying to get in, someone else goes down ahead of me.

Then Jesus said to him, "Get up! Pick up your mat and walk." At once the man was cured; he picked up his mat and walked.

The day on which this took place was a Sabbath, and so the Jewish leaders said to the man who had been healed, "It is the Sabbath; the law forbids you to carry your mat."

But he replied, "The man who made me well said to me, 'Pick up your mat and walk.'"

So they asked him, "Who is this fellow who told you to pick it up and walk?"

The man who was healed had no idea who it was, for Jesus had slipped away into the crowd that was there.

Later Jesus found him at the temple and said to him, "See, you are well again. Stop sinning or something worse may happen to you." The man went away and told the Jews that it was Jesus who had made him well.

JOHN 5: 5-15 (NIV)

The invalid at the pool of Bethesda, who is healed from nearly a lifetime of illness, is the quintessential ingrate. He intentionally seeks out the Pharisees in order to identify Jesus as the one who helped heal him on the Sabbath—which was a violation of rabbinical law. It is clear this will mean trouble for Jesus. The invalid represents the shadow side of the contracted heart, something lurking as a destructive potential in human unconsciousness. He also speaks to the past and the culture from which he comes. The author of the Gospel of John reveals his own biases by presenting a story about the rigid practices of the Pharisees and their irrational influence on the people. We would be missing something, however, to read this story only as a troubling indictment of a group of people with differing religious views. In this story the author is attempting to distinguish his own preferred spirituality, which is Christ-centered—an ineffable, mystical, boundless faith—from old religious rigid laws and rituals. For the author of John, Christ represents dissolution of the egoic "I" into the supreme identity of the Christ. Jesus has surrendered personal will and identity to Alaha: Sacred Unity. "I and the Father are One." (John 10:20 NIV)

The man at the pool has a lot to teach us. Although he has had access to the healing waters of life for many years, he cannot manage to avail himself to the spiritual renewal offered to him. We would do well to take a good look at this man. We all have the potential to assume an identity defined by our limitations and a lifetime of excuses, and once they are exposed, to turn against those who try to help us. The man at the pool is infuriating, and he is also a powerful teacher. He carries the burden for us of the contracted heart and constricted mind. By negative example he teaches us how to correct our own course in life.

The unnamed man has spent a lifetime before a pool of healing potential. Everything he needs to restore him is at his feet. Most likely his meager subsistence is sustained by the charity of others. Unlike the hemorrhagic woman— who also appears in the Gospel of John and who will stop at nothing to reach her healing goal—this man languishes in excuses. Jesus poses the question, "Do you want to get well?" What follows is typical of our human response when confronted with the kind of probing inquiry that cuts right to the core of our issues. He deflects the question with a habitual and well-used litany of excuses. No one will help him. The timing is all wrong. Because of his exceptional circumstances and dire predicament, he misses opportunities for healing when they arise. Jesus sees through this man's self-deception right away. In his book, *The Gospel of John in the Light of Indian Mysticism*, Ravi Ravindra notes that in this story the ego holds prominence, and this unfortunate man, "cannot place himself in the right relationship to the truth."[73] What a shock it must be for him to hear Jesus command: "Pick up your mat and walk!" The others who are gathered at the pool witness the exchange between Jesus and the invalid. They know the man well and are all too familiar with his situation. They might have wanted to tell him the same thing for years. In this scene, the artful and commanding nature of the Christ shows up as clear, concise, and compassionate communication that powerfully calls us on our victimhood. A powerful intervention such as this can shake us out of our old identity in such a way that we pick ourselves and our old story up and take notice—like the man at the pool.

According to some scientists, there is something termed a "positivity offset." This is a slightly more positive than a negative outlook toward the everyday events of our lives. We also can shift into a negative reaction when we experience a major life event. This reaction can be beneficial when it helps us evaluate the safest course through a difficult time. However, if we tend to gravitate toward a generally negative outlook on life, it makes it extremely difficult to experience gratitude for the good things that come our way. Complaints and resentments become habitual, perhaps even addictive, because we cannot face our lives without the drama of our complaints.

Our ungrateful friend at the pool in Bethesda might be infuriating, but he also warrants our compassion. What an agony it must be to not recognize when we are blessed. How miserable to be unable to accept a good deed when it comes to us. He has experienced many difficult challenges in his life, and he feels overcome by them. He lacks a foundation in consciousness to support a change for the better. At a deep and tender level, he might feel that he is unworthy. He could be frightened. He has over-identified with what the Buddhists and Eastern philosophies call the "small self," at the expense of experiencing a greater sense of spiritual freedom. This is a tragedy of the human condition.

When the man is healed from his malady, he picks up his mat and leaves, but then he is stopped and confronted with violating the Sabbath. Jewish law prohibits any activity construed as work on the Sabbath, and carrying his mat fits into this category. The man tells the Pharisees he was ordered to carry his mat by someone he did not recognize.

He is unable to claim responsibility for carrying his mat or rejoice in his ability to do so. "The man who made me well said to...," he replied. There is no indication he appreciates his gift of healing. He seeks to avoid responsibility for breaking the law by pointing an accusing finger. Blame is toxic and it poisons any possible outpouring of a grateful heart. One cannot be grateful and blaming at the same time. He succumbs to his old familiar role of helplessness. Of course the man does not know who helped him heal. He cannot recognize the Christ. He is not open to Christ consciousness. Ingratitude is itself an accusation.[74]

Later, Jesus finds the man at the temple and assures him he is now well. Jesus also offers him a stern warning: "Stop sinning or something worse may happen to you." Jesus uses the word "sin," an archery term meaning to "miss the mark." He instructs the man to correct the course of his life. Sin is a state of mind and action when we think and act as if we are separate from God. The man at the pool will need to accept what it means to be whole and commit to his renewal, or his predicament will be even worse. If we are unable to turn away from self-deception, victimization, and blame, we will return to our former misery. Our experience will be even more distressing once we experience a taste of freedom from our suffering.

In an action that illustrates the basest form of ingratitude, the man betrays the Christ and informs against him, the one who made his healing possible. "The man went away and told the Jews that it was Jesus who had made him well." The sixteenth century Saint Ignatius of Loyola wrote, "It seems to me that ingratitude is the most abominable of sins.... It is a forgetting of the graces, benefits and blessing received, and as such it is the cause, beginning and origin of all sins and misfortunes."[75] Like Narcissus, who falls in love with his reflection in the water, our man at the pool is a drowning man, lost in his egoic identification with his problems, limitations, and bias toward blame. His example provides a stern warning for all of us to make whatever corrections are necessary in our own self-perceptions to avoid such a tragic course.

REFLECTIONS & QUESTIONS

1. Sometimes we learn by negative example, as in the case of the man at the pool of Bethesda. As a shadow figure, it is useful to bring him into the light and take a good look, because, except for grace and wisdom, we all have the potential to take on an identity defined by our limitations and excuses.
What is helpful to you in the example of the man at the pool? How have you learned from the negative example of others?

2. Cultivating gratitude seems to help us in our everyday life. Yet sometimes, when things are going well for us, we say things like, "I wonder when the other shoe will drop." We wonder if we can afford the luxury of gratefulness.
Reflect on the difference between experiencing a purely grateful heart and one in which we question if we can "afford" to be grateful.

3. Once we recognize how limiting our old ways of thinking are, we are empowered to make better choices and decisions. If we get stuck in blaming our traditions and culture, or others, we tend to remain victims.
How have you healed some of the misunderstandings you were taught? What do you find of value in some of the old teachings you have outgrown?

Ruth Ann Lonardelli

There is Work to Do: Born Blind

A s he went along, he saw a man blind from birth. His disciples asked him, "Rabbi, who sinned, this man or his parents, that he was born blind?"

"Neither this man nor his parents sinned," said Jesus, "but this happened so that the works of God might be displayed in him. As long as it is day, we must do the works of him who sent me. Night is coming, when no one can work. While I am in the world, I am the light of the world."

After saying this, he spit on the ground, made some mud with the saliva, and put it on the man's eyes. "Go," he told him, "wash in the Pool of Siloam" (this word means "Sent"). So the man went and washed, and came home seeing.

His neighbors and those who had formerly seen him begging asked, "Isn't this the same man who used to sit and beg?" Some claimed that he was. Others said, "No, he only looks like him." But he himself insisted, "I am the man."

"How then were your eyes opened?" they asked.

He replied, "The man they call Jesus made some mud and put it on my eyes. He told me to go to Siloam and wash. So I went and washed, and then I could see."

"Where is this man?" they asked him. "I don't know," he said.

They brought to the Pharisees the man who had been blind. Now the day on which Jesus had made the mud and

opened the man's eyes was a Sabbath. Therefore the Pharisees also asked him how he had received his sight. "He put
mud on my eyes," the man replied, "and I washed, and now
I see."

Some of the Pharisees said, "This man is not from God,
for he does not keep the Sabbath." But others asked, "How can
a sinner perform such signs?" So they were divided.

Then they turned again to the blind man, "What have
you to say about him? It was your eyes he opened."

The man replied, "He is a prophet." They still did not
believe that he had been blind and had received his sight
until they sent for the man's parents. "Is this your son?" they
asked. "Is this the one you say was born blind? How is it that
now he can see?"

"We know he is our son," the parents answered, "and we
know he was born blind. But how he can see now, or who
opened his eyes, we don't know. Ask him. He is of age; he will
speak for himself." His parents said this because they were
afraid of the Jewish leaders, who already had decided that
anyone who acknowledged that Jesus was the Messiah would
be put out of the synagogue. That was why his parents said,
"He is of age; ask him."

A second time they summoned the man who had been
blind. "Give glory to God by telling the truth," they said. "We
know this man is a sinner."

He replied, "Whether he is a sinner or not, I don't know.
One thing I do know. I was blind but now I see!"

Then they asked him, "What did he do to you? How did
he open your eyes?"

He answered, "I have told you already and you did not
listen. Why do you want to hear it again? Do you want to
become his disciples too?"

Then they hurled insults at him and said, "You are this fellow's disciple! We are disciples of Moses! We know that God spoke to Moses, but as for this fellow, we don't even know where he comes from."

The man answered, "Now that is remarkable! You don't know where he comes from, yet he opened my eyes. We know that God does not listen to sinners. He listens to the godly person who does his will. Nobody has ever heard of opening the eyes of a man born blind. If this man were not from God, he could do nothing."

To this they replied, "You were steeped in sin at birth; how dare you lecture us!" And they threw him out.

Jesus heard that they had thrown him out, and when he found him, he said, "Do you believe in the Son of Man?"

"Who is he, sir?" the man asked. "Tell me so that I may believe in him."

Jesus said, "You have now seen him; in fact, he is the one speaking with you."

Then the man said, "Lord, I believe," and he worshiped him.

Jesus said, "For judgment I have come into this world, so that the blind will see and those who see will become blind."

Some Pharisees who were with him heard him say this and asked, "What? Are we blind too?"

Jesus said, "If you were blind, you would not be guilty of sin; but now that you claim you can see, your guilt remains."

JOHN 9:13-41 (NIV)

THIS MAN HAS BEEN BLIND SINCE BIRTH, AND HIS PRE-
dicament is the subject of a complex discourse that plays
out with a panoply of characters and changing scenes. At
the heart of the discussion is the perplexing question of why
bad things happen to good people. Do we blame ourselves,
or are we tainted by the misdeeds of our families? "Rabbi,"
the disciples ask Jesus, "Who sinned, this man or his parents,
that he was born blind?" To what extent are we personally
responsible for the horrible suffering we endure?

We have a human propensity to want to know why. This
is an easy question to ask and often impossible to answer.
It is one of the first questions we ask as young children.
These are the kinds of questions that spring innocently
and spontaneously from our struggle to make sense of life.
"Why?" a young child will ask about almost anything. After
a while, we stop asking. Things either start to make sense,
or we give up trying to make sense of it all. But questions
about the cause of disease and suffering are never far from
our consciousness. Whenever we witness or experience
difficult challenges in life, we return to asking, "Who or
what is responsible for this and *why*?"

Jesus' response is that no one is responsible for what
caused the man's blindness. "Neither this man nor his parents sinned." He goes on to say, "But this happened so that
the work of God might be displayed in his life. As long as
it is day, we must do the work of him who sent me."

Jesus answers the question about the culpability of
the parents and the blind man, absolving them of responsibility for the situation. That is, neither the sins of the
past or present account for this condition nor does Jesus
blame God. Speculating about cause can only take us so
far. Ascribing blame provides little satisfaction and will

never fulfill our need to make peace with suffering. From theological musings about the cause of the man's suffering, Jesus moves swiftly toward action. He says we have work to do. There might not be intrinsic meaning in the suffering itself; however, how we respond to suffering is meaningful. Hence, healing happens, the amelioration of suffering occurs through us at work in the world. We become the hands and service of God. Margaret Wheatley, author and teacher, writes, "Action, like a sacrament, is the visible form of an invisible spirit, an outward manifestation of an inward power."[76] Acts of compassion and service spontaneously arise as a natural expression of an inner state of oneness and connection with our sacred source and with each other.

The stumbling block in this conversation among the Pharisees is an infantile attachment to an old world God who erratically metes out illness and dispenses cures. The God of Jesus is not a superhuman in the sky. This kind of understanding harkens back to the ancient Greeks, whose gods were capricious, easily swayed by the actions and petitions of humanity, and in perpetual need of appeasement. The God of Jesus is immanent and integral, the ineffable, inherent mystery of spirit, love, compassion, and wholeness. What Jesus is teaching here is that spiritual blindness is healed when we begin to see from an awareness of God as Sacred Source. Then we see with spiritual clarity, rather than in just a surface sense.

"'Go,' he told him, 'wash in the Pool of Siloam.' So the man went and washed, and came home seeing."

The course of treatment prescribed by Jesus combines the most earthy and natural of cures with an instruction for the patient. Jesus applies a poultice for the blind man's condition. He "...spit on the ground, made some mud with the saliva and put it on the man's eyes." Using saliva as a way to clean wounds is an ancient, universal remedy. In the humble fluids of life there are properties that act as antibiotics or antivirals and serve medicinal purposes. In the simple application of mud and spittle, Jesus affirms the healing energies in life itself, in Mother Earth. Somewhere in the world today, you will find an attentive mother spitting on her finger and wiping her child's face or tending to a scrape. The call of care inevitably leads to getting our hands dirty.

Then Jesus instructs the man to go wash in the Pool of Siloam. This is an important step in the healing process. The healing does not only depend on the healer. Taking responsibility for our health is an important component of our healing. Rather than blaming others or ourselves, we are required to take personal action and move toward the healing waters with a purposeful intention and goal. Once the blind man follows the instruction and takes action, his sight is restored.

The message in this story is clearly revealed. Spiritual insights are right here where we are. We are required to act, to move forward until we can see them. Look around you. The immanent presence of the divine is found within life itself, and in the gifts of Mother Earth.

In this story, the blind man who is restored to sight recognizes the presence of the Christ. He is deeply grateful. "Give Glory to God," he says. He expresses his gratitude by standing firm in his experience despite the pressure to be drawn into distracting arguments and accusations. This stands in contrast to the preceding story in John about the paralytic man who was healed at the Pool of Bethesda. The man was healed from his malady; however, he did not integrate the experience into a deeper personal understanding and spiritual growth. He not only remained ungrateful, he also reported Jesus to the Pharisees. These two contrasting stories demonstrate a choice. Which approach is most likely to result in a more authentic experience of spiritual healing? We can choose to be chronically dissatisfied and disgruntled victims, or we can choose to explore what is possible and take the necessary actions. We can also be grateful for the insights that come to us in the process.

Other characters in this story come to the front of the stage. They engage in a discussion about what they have witnessed. Some question the man was ever blind. These are the doubts we ourselves experience when we learn of the seemingly miraculous, inexplicable healing of others. Some find fault with the method. It is not the "standard of care." In the Jewish tradition, non-threatening illnesses were not treated on the Sabbath. To do so violated laws that prohibited working on that day.

A debate ensues among the Pharisees and the newly sighted man. He has been blind all his life and now he sees! Those who are blind to this great transformation hurl insults, and, eventually, they dismiss him altogether.

In the final scene, Jesus learns the newly-sighted man has been tossed out by the Pharisees, and he goes to find him. Perhaps Jesus finds the man standing mesmerized by the dappled light or spellbound by a reflection in the surface of the pool. The whole world is alive for him in a new way—colors, contours, and shadows, as well as deepening spiritual sensibility. Jesus affirms what the man's physical and refined spiritual senses tell him. The Christ is not separate from his experience. It is a profound breakthrough in awareness when he recognizes the presence of the sacred in the concerns of his life.

A few Pharisees hang around to hear what Jesus will say. To them he says, "If you were blind, you would not be guilty of sin; but now that you claim you can see, your guilt remains." This wisdom teaching is ancient, and it appears in many mystical teachings. From the Hindu Vedas comes the insight that Brahman, the Supreme Cosmic Spirit, is a mystery beyond understanding, eternal, both immanent and transcendent. It is not possible to describe or define Brahman, or God. Such an undertaking would be the height of hubris and misunderstanding. All of our best theologies and philosophies fail to grasp *It*. Metaphorically speaking, if you were born blind—meaning you are oblivious to superficial things and are not deluded by your own God-knowledge and believe you have all the answers—then you have inner vision, insight into God's indefinable nature. However, "…that you claim you can see, your guilt remains." In other words, if you think you know who or what God is, then you have failed to grasp the meaning. The wisdom teaching is that God is beyond the superfluous laws and theologies of the Pharisees.

Before we become too dismissive of the Pharisees, it is worthwhile to note we all exhibit similar tendencies from time to time. The author of John uses the Pharisees as an example personifying the human proclivity to show up as defensive know-it-alls, relying on backup from all our acquired knowledge and traditions to conceal our hardened hearts and limited vision. We would miss the point of these stories entirely if we castigate a group of people such as the Pharisees, when it is our own shadows, our egos and self-righteousness that need to be brought into the light. Our own vision needs to be restored so we can see with a deeper awareness, and from this awareness do the work of service and healing in the world.

REFLECTIONS & QUESTIONS

1. In our efforts to understand why suffering happens, we ask unanswerable questions. Sometimes we resort to ascribing blame. Even if someone is culpable, and we are able to identify the wrong and obtain human justice, we might still be left with many unanswered questions. We tend to recycle the unanswerable "why."
   How does taking action create meaning and peace? What does being caught in the "why" create instead?

2. Spiritual insights are right here where we are, in the very basics of life itself.
   What does this statement mean? How might we expand our awareness so we can notice what spiritual insights are readily available to us?

3. We can choose to be chronically dissatisfied and self-serving, or we can choose to explore what other possibilities and actions are available to us now.
   Reflect on actions you have taken and choices you have made in the past. What are some choices and actions you wish to take now?

Ruth Ann Lonardelli

The Womb of the Great Mother: The Woman at the Well

I t was about the sixth hour. When a Samaritan woman came to draw water, Jesus said to her, "Will you give me a drink?" (His disciples had gone into the town to buy food.)

The Samaritan woman said to him, "You are a Jew and I am a Samaritan woman. How can you ask me for a drink?" (For Jews do not associate with Samaritans.)

Jesus answered her, "If you knew the gift of God and who it is that asks you for a drink you would have asked him and he would have given you living water."

"Everyone who drinks this water will be thirsty again, but whoever drinks the water I give him will never thirst. Indeed, the water I give him will become in him like a spring of water welling up to eternal life."

The woman said to him, "Sir, give me this water so that I won't get thirsty and have to keep coming here to draw water."

He told her, "Go, call your husband and come back."

"I have no husband, she replied."

Jesus said to her, "You are right when you say you have no husband. The fact is, you have had five husbands, and the man you now have is not your husband....God is spirit, and his worshipers must worship in the Spirit and in truth."

Then, leaving her water jar, the woman went back to the town and said to the people, "Come, see a man who told me everything I ever did. Could this be the Messiah?"

Many of the Samaritans from that town believed in him because of the woman's testimony.

JOHN 4:6B-10,13-18,24, 28-29, 39 (NIV)

⸺⸻⸺

THE WOMAN AT THE WELL WAS A FIRST-CENTURY SAMARitan woman from the town of Synchar, and on that day, much like any other day, she came to draw water at the sixth hour for her household from the community well. There she encountered the Jewish teacher. He was traveling back to Galilee from Judea, and despite the preferences of some of his companions, he had chosen to enter Samaritan territory.

Even though Samaritans and Jews worshiped the same God, tensions existed between the two groups, most notably related to the distinct differences in how and where they worshiped. The community well in this story was a meeting place where these differences lost their significance. Here is a convergence of our shared human needs, which is essential for a healthy physical and spiritual life. This well could be an attribution to Jacob's well, a reference connecting readers with an old story from the Hebrew tradition. In that story, the well was the meeting place where Jacob first met his beloved Rachael.

The symbolism of the well is also more universal and timeless, and its relevance cannot be restricted to one group of people at one particular time and place. Wells are sustaining, nurturing channels of life emerging from the earth.

Although functional and vital to life, there is a quality of mystery about them. They open out into the light and at the same time disappear into dark chambers of the unknown. They retain a feminine quality associated with the womb of Mother Earth. The water they bring offers life-giving substance, but there is also ancient spiritual meaning in observances that honor the feminine aspects of creation.

The well in ancient cultures marked a common meeting place where people mingled to listen to the latest gossip and share in the life of the community. Life-giving water serves as a place for connection. Jesus stopped at this place to rest, while his companions went in search of food for the journey ahead. The nameless woman and Jesus meet at the well, and Jesus asks her for a drink of water. He is thirsty and does not have the vessel he needs to dip into the reservoir and draw out a drink. In his request there is the moving recognition of the commonality of our basic needs and our need for each other. At the core of our human experience, we are more similar than dissimilar. The recognition of our common human needs draws us all closer together, regardless of the boundaries of cultures and religions, just as it brings these two unlikely characters into a life-altering encounter.

At first, when Jesus addresses the woman, she is startled. How is it, she asks, a Jew would ask a Samaritan for a drink? It is even more unusual for a Jewish male to be engaged in a conversation with any woman, much less a Samaritan, in public. Then Jesus shifts the conversation from the ordinary water of everyday life to the "living water" that quenches our deep spiritual thirst. The woman strains to understand the symbolic meaning of his words. At first she takes him literally, missing the point that he is talking about spiritual awakening and timeless fulfillment. Jesus explains this "water" is not of the material world or external to ourselves, but rather it is an indwelling sacred source of regeneration flowing from the living wellspring within us.

The woman at the well is a multilayered character. She is a reflection of the complex structure of the Gospel of John. In contrast to the sayings and parables of the synoptic gospels, John's gospel contains many long and perplexing discourses inviting multiple interpretations.

On one level, she represents our shared humanness, regardless of gender, seeking to meet the needs of everyday life. The exchange between Jesus and the woman continues. Jesus prods her personal past and reveals that he knows about her multiple marriages. He knows the man who is with her now is not her husband. The number of past husbands and her present companion adds up to six. From the lens of traditional interpretation, we are led to understand that this woman was someone who had a scandalous past. In a culture in which divorce is not only disallowed and adultery a cause for a death by stoning, her circumstances are even more complex. Rather than living a life without scruples, she is someone who has suffered multiple difficulties and challenges. Perhaps she has been widowed many times, or she has been a slave with many masters. When this woman comes to the well of rejuvenation, she is carrying more than an empty vessel. Like all of us, she carries her past with all its heartaches, losses, and disappointments.

The conversation between the two of them continues. It is an astonishing exchange. Jesus engages in a deep, profound dialogue with a nameless, life-weary woman. This is the kind of conversation more typical among equals. Jesus comments that our everyday physical need for water reflects a spiritual counterpart—our longing to tap into the wellspring of the Christ presence, the realization of the sacred within our ordinary lives. This water is the fulfillment of our thirst, our yearning for connection with our spiritual source. The woman responds with interest. "Sir," she says, "give me some of that water, so that I may never get thirsty and never have to come here again." In her response there is the weariness of her life, with its endless concerns, cares, and burdens of the past. In this way, she is everywoman, beset by the seemingly endless demands of life. Our common shared humanity shows up in her simple wish for respite.

At the culmination of the encounter, Jesus presents the radical notion that it is now time for authentic worship in spirit and truth, an understanding that departs from traditional temple worship. Like water overflowing its container, this kind of worship cannot be contained, but expresses in life wherever we are. This is a transformative teaching. At the end of her discussion with Jesus, the woman abandons her vessel, because what has been shared here cannot be contained or conveyed in any material way. She returns to her community with the story of her experience. It is interesting to note the townspeople are attentive to her and believe her experience. If she had been an individual with compromised status in her community, a condemned woman with a shameful past, certainly no one would have found her encounter at the well particularly credible. The response of the townspeople to her message is an indication she is respected and she does have influence. The people of Synchar listen to her, and as a result they come to meet Jesus and listen to what he is teaching. The disciples return to the well to meet with Jesus, and they find him talking to a Samaritan woman. Unlike the earlier Jesus who attempted to turn away a foreign woman seeking healing for her child, this Jesus has reached beyond the limitations of tribal consciousness to connect deeply with another from a different group.

Jesus has been instructing his disciples for many months, but most of them still do not understand what he is saying. In contrast, the woman at the well moved quickly from a literal understanding of his teaching into a higher level of understanding. She realized this was a transformative message of heart and spirit—the realization of a deep truth.

There are many ancient depictions of the goddess carrying vessels to draw up water for the needs of the people, or to dispense mercy and compassion. The number six, cited first in the time of day when Jesus arrives at the well, the sixth hour, and again in the number of men in the woman's life, is the number associated with Aphrodite, the Greek goddess of love. The well, the womb of Great Mother, is the place where the beleaguered and marginalized feminine encounters the Christ. What happens here is an enactment of sacred reconnection.[77] The immanent and transcendent meet. The nameless woman at the well carries the burden of a maligned history and the weariness of earthly experience. She is welcomed and included into the conversation by the Christ. Her presence warrants respect. She is worthy of sacred knowledge. She receives insight and she shares it with her community. From an ordinary cup of water, a symbol of life on Earth, the miracle of a new and complete creation emerges—the awakening of a consciousness of wholeness embracing the wisdom of the indwelling immanent and the infinite vision of the transcendent.

Ruth Ann Lonardelli

REFLECTIONS & QUESTIONS

1. At the core of our human experience, we are more similar than dissimilar. The recognition of our common human needs and life experiences draws us into the fold of connection. *How does the awareness of our commonly shared experiences and needs affect how you feel about yourself in relationship to others?*

2. When we move from a literal understanding of a spiritual teaching into a higher level of understanding, there is a transformative message of spirit and the realization of a deep truth. *What is your experience of the difference between literal meaning and spiritual meaning?*

Touching the Ground of Being: "Neither Do I Condemn You"

J esus went to the Mount of Olives. At dawn he appeared
again in the temple courts, where all the people gathered around him, and he sat down to teach them. The
teachers of the law and the Pharisees brought in a woman
caught in adultery. They made her stand before the group
and said to Jesus, "Teacher, this woman was caught in
the act of adultery. In the Law Moses commanded us to
stone such women. Now what do you say?" They were
using the question to trap him, in order to have a basis
for accusing him.

But Jesus bent down and started to write on the ground
with his finger. When they kept on questioning him, he
straightened up and said to them, "Let any one of you who
is without sin be the first to throw a stone at her." Again he
stooped down and wrote on the ground.

At this, those who heard began to go away one at a
time, the older ones first, until only Jesus was left with
the woman still standing there. Jesus straightened up and
asked her, "Woman, where are they? Has no one condemned you?"

"No one, sir," she said.

"Then neither do I condemn you," Jesus declared. "Go now and leave your life of sin."

JOHN 8:1-11 (NIV)

⌘

THE FATE OF THIS WOMAN WAS PRESCRIBED BY THE LAW: death by stoning. The edict was clear; however, how and when the law was applied is less certain. We do not know what the actual penalties for adultery were at the time this story was originally told. This scene is a fragment, written by someone other than the author of John, and inserted into the eighth chapter of the gospel at some later time. Biblical scholars think this piece was added 400-500 years after the original manuscript was written. This might have been a familiar story that was circulating orally and then finally captured in these passages. We do know adultery was considered an offense; however, sometimes such indictments served as heavily weighted threats intended to maintain proper conduct in community life. Whatever the actual practices were, the accusers of this story seem prepared to carry out the sentence.

The Pharisees and teachers of the law are using the woman as bait. She is stripped of her humanity. She is not regarded as a daughter, a friend, or a lover. This unnamed woman is merely another temptation to dangle in front of Jesus and test his ministry. It takes two to commit adultery, but she alone bears the guilt of the adulterous act, as well as the shame. She is standing before a court of angry men along with a crowd of people who have come to hear Jesus' teaching that day. Her accusers testify that she was caught in the act. This would fulfill the requirement of the law for witnesses to substantiate the crime of adultery. Everything is now in order for the sentence to be carried out.

The wisdom of this story is in Jesus' call for self-inquiry. Who is innocent among us? From Jesus' teachings in Matthew, we know his position on adultery is clear. Not only is he opposed to adultery, he says that whoever looks at another with lust has committed the act already. Guilt or innocence is not the issue here; however, our strident defensiveness and self-righteousness are called into question. In this remarkable, tiny story fragment, the author goes straight to the heart of our human inclination to place ourselves in a more positive light than we perceive in others, and to project onto others more negative traits. Such projections can easily escalate. They carry the potential to incite violence, torture, and death.

A stoning death is merciless torture. In the Jewish tradition, the accused was thrown down from a high precipice, a large stone was dropped on top of the accused, and he or she was then pelted with rocks. The stones needed to be big enough to cause painful injury leading to death, but small enough so the ordeal would be drawn out. In a stoning, it is not always certain which rock delivers the death. In this way, no one can be singled out as the one responsible for the deathblow. This is an unspoken, collective agreement about how to avoid responsibility for taking a life. In contrast to the one solitary woman standing accountable for the transgression of adultery, the mob is absolved of any individual responsibility for the act of torture and killing. Torture is then justified as simply a fulfillment of the law.

The story begins at dawn. Jesus returns from the Mount of Olives to teach. These evocative details are precise indicators of the consciousness of this teacher. Daybreak symbolizes enlightenment and clarity. Out of the incubation of darkness, a new day shines through. Jesus has been on the mountain again—a landscape depicted many times in the gospel stories as a place of expanded awareness and wisdom consciousness. From this higher perspective, Jesus comes to teach. He is backlit by imagery of enlightened, breakthrough awareness.

Jesus responds in two rather remarkable ways when he is confronted with the accused and the accusers. First, he says nothing. Instead of responding with a lengthy discourse or defensiveness, he demonstrates wisdom by creating a wedge of silence in this potentially volatile scene. He understands that he and the woman are both on trial here. He realizes the potential exists to create a teaching moment to serve and enlighten others. Jesus bends down and touches the ground and traces his fingers in the earth. There has been much speculation about this act. What could this gesture mean? Some researchers believe the whole scene was contrived to support the dubious presupposition that Jesus knew how to write. Others suggest he was scribbling signs that would identify the accusers in the crowd who were guilty of similar crimes. Tracing his fingers into the earth is an unusual gesture and not like any other in the stories of Jesus. It is, however, much like a scene in the Buddhist tradition.

The story is that Buddha was seated under the Bodhi tree when he obtained enlightenment. As a final temptation, the great tempter Mara and his army appeared to Buddha and challenged his enlightened state of being. In response, Buddha touched the ground with the fingertips of his right hand. This was a subtle and powerful moment. Rather than a confrontational response to his challenge, the Buddha's gesture grounded him in a deeper sense of connection and peace. When the earth responded with a shudder in recognition of the Buddha and as an affirmation of his awakened presence, his tempters vanished.

Jesus stoops, touches, and writes on the ground. In this way, he also touched the source of wisdom, which informs his response. His action is but the slightest disruption in the escalating violence, allowing him enough time to reach even deeper into his Christ consciousness. He connects with Mother Earth and finds the inspiration, guidance, and just the right words to transform this potentially dangerous situation into a peaceful and insightful resolution. Jesus stands up and says to them, "If any one of you is without sin, let him be the first to throw a stone at her." Then he stoops and writes on the ground once more. Again, it is an elegantly simple gesture that breaks the momentum of violence. As his gaze is directed away from the accusers, they are not singled out in blame. One by one, the accusers move away. When he stands up again, they have all left. Like Buddha's tempters, Mara and his entourage, the accusers have dispersed. The only one remaining is the woman. To her he says, "Woman, where are they? Has no one condemned you?" "No one, sir," she says. "Then neither do I condemn you," Jesus declares. "Go now and leave your life of sin." Jesus is not justifying wrongdoing and poor choices. He understands there are enough bad judgments and wrong decisions to go around. He is teaching us to accept responsibility for our own actions and judgments before resorting to accusations that could escalate into violence.

Jesus and the Buddha draw wisdom and strength from their connection with their spiritual source; they resist the temptation to react defensively. Rather than reacting, they connect with the ground of all being and their spiritual core. This allows them to respond with wisdom, compassion, and temperance.

REFLECTIONS & QUESTIONS

1. Sometimes silence and resisting the temptation to become verbally defensive is the best response to a threatening situation. When we become defensive about our positions, our hearts harden. Our rigidity also incites others and problems can escalate. It is a powerful temptation to offer a verbal defense. It requires a lot of internal reserve to let the temptation pass.

   Have you noticed what happens for you and others when you are tempted to defend your position verbally? How does it feel to let the impulse to react defensively pass? Describe the actual feelings in your body at the various stages of such an encounter. Where do you experience defensiveness in your body when you feel on the spot?

   How might it feel to take enough time to connect with your center before speaking? How does it feel when the situation is behind you and you resist becoming defensive?

2. A mob mentality can absolve us of individual responsibly and justify violent acts.

   As a nation, how do we abdicate responsibility for the way others are treated? Reflect on the implications of forfeiting a sense of responsibility for collective violence and imagine other possibilities.

The Dark Night of the Soul: Lazarus

*T*he sisters [Martha and Mary] sent word to Jesus, "Lord, the one you love is sick."

When he heard this, Jesus said, "This sickness will not end in death...."

Now Jesus loved Martha and her sister and Lazarus. So when he heard that Lazarus was sick, he stayed where he was two more days, and then he said to his disciples, "Let us go back to Judea."

On his arrival, Jesus found that Lazarus had already been in the tomb for four days. Now Bethany was less than two miles from Jerusalem, and many Jews had come to Martha and Mary to comfort them in the loss of their brother. When Martha heard that Jesus was coming, she went out to meet him, but Mary stayed at home.

"Lord," Martha said to Jesus, "if you had been here, my brother would not have died. But I know that even now God will give you whatever you ask."

Jesus said to her, "Your brother will rise again."

Martha answered, "I know he will rise again in the resurrection at the last day."

Jesus said to her, "I am the resurrection and the life. The one who believes in me will live, even though he dies, and whoever dies and believes in me will never die. Do you believe this?"

"Yes, Lord," she told him, "I believe that you are the Messiah, the Son of God, who is to come into the world."

When Mary reached the place where Jesus was and saw him, she fell at his feet and said, "Lord, if you had been here, my brother would not have died."

When Jesus saw her weeping, and the Jews who had come along with her also weeping, he was deeply moved in spirit and troubled. "Where have you laid him?" he asked.

"Come and see, Lord," they replied. Jesus wept.

Then the Jews said, "See how he loved him!"

Jesus, once more deeply moved, came to the tomb. It was a cave with a stone laid across the entrance. "Take away the stone," he said..... So they took away the stone. Then Jesus looked up and said, "Father, I thank you that you have heard me. I knew that you always hear me, but I said this for the benefit of the people standing here, that they may believe that you sent me."

When he had said this, Jesus called in a loud voice, "Lazarus come out!" The dead man came out, his hands and feet wrapped with strips of linen and a cloth around his face.

Jesus said to them, "Take off the grave clothes and let him go."

JOHN 11: 3-4A, 5-7, 17-27, 32-36, 38-39A, 41-44 (NIV)

⸻

THE RAISING OF LAZARUS FROM THE DEAD IS A WELL-known story from the Gospel of John. This story contains evocative entreaties, a measured response, outcomes deliberately paced, and the nested foreshadowing of the even more dramatic death and resurrection scene that is to come.

Jesus has left Judea—a place where he met with difficulty and threats. He is summoned back by his friends Martha and Mary to assist their gravely ill brother, Lazarus. Jesus does not respond right away. "This sickness will not end in death," he says with assurance, and then he waits another two days before he returns to them.

This is not unlike the times when our fervent prayers for help are accompanied by the expectation that help will come swiftly. The answers we are seeking often arrive in their own time and in their own way. It is a troubling and anxious wait. If you have ever waited for a doctor to show up, or waited for the results of medical tests, or held vigil for a loved one in the waiting room of a hospital, you know how the pitch of anxiety eventually tangles with faith. There must be someone who can help, someone who can tell us what to do. Where are they? This is the deafening silence we experience when it seems our prayers have not been answered in the way we wish, and the help we counted on is not there.

Added to their concerns about Lazarus are concerns about the welfare of their friend and teacher, Jesus. Why has he not come? He could have met with difficulties as well, and in these waiting hours the human mind leaps and lunges at the escalating worries so typical of our highly stressed lives. The sisters—for all their devotion and faith—and Lazarus experience a dark night of the soul in which Lazarus succumbs. These are the ones of whom it is said, "Jesus loved Martha and her sister and Lazarus." Not even love, devotion, or faith can shield us from the suffering of life.

Jesus finally arrives. Lazarus has been dead for four days. The author of John wants us to know that Lazarus' situation is hopeless. He is beyond any help. There is nothing that can be done now. Martha is the first to greet Jesus. "If you had been here," she says, "my brother would not have died." Martha speaks for all of us. When we are exhausted, when we have been kept hoping and waiting for help to come, recriminations are the first words likely to come out of us when help does arrive. How quickly this edginess and the long agony and frustration of waiting passes when hope is restored!

"But I know that even now God will give you whatever you ask," says Martha. She is the first to recognize what Jesus affirms when he says, "Your brother will rise again…. Do you believe this?"

"Yes," says Martha. I believe that you are the Christ…."

Mary also hears that Jesus has arrived, and she runs out to meet him. In a scene similar to the encounter between Martha and Jesus, Mary says, "Lord, if you had been here, my brother would not have died."

These responses of Mary and Martha give voice to what we sometimes feel when we are faced with challenges and tragedies. "Where were you, God? Where is God?" Like the deafening silence that follows such a question, Jesus does not offer a litany of excuses, explanations, or defensiveness. Jesus responds by listening.

Holocaust survivor and author Elie Wiesel tells of witnessing the horrors in a Nazi concentration camp. In the midst of a particularly tragic scene, he heard someone call out, "For God's sake, where is God?" Then from deep within Wiesel says, "I heard a voice answer: "Where He is? This is where…."[78] He is weeping, suffering, and dying with us.

When Jesus finds Mary weeping, and the Jews who had come with her weeping as well, he is deeply moved in spirit and troubled.

"Where have you laid him?" he asks. "Come and see, Lord," they reply. Jesus wept. Then the Jews said, See how he loved him!"

"Jesus wept." This is shortest sentence in the gospel stories. These two words disclose the compassionate, immanent presence of the sacred, which suffers with us in the darkest moments of our lives. In this timeless, poignant scene, the empathic Heart of God grieves, weeping with friends and the community. In the end, it is God who suffers, dies again and again, and who is eternally reborn.

The sorrow of Martha and Mary is not unlike that of Isis and Nephthys, two goddesses of Egypt. Isis and her sister Nephthys mourn the death of their beloved brother Osiris. They, too, seek a way to restore him to life. They embark on a long ordeal of healing and restoration, and through their efforts Osiris is revived. Although similar, there are important differences between these two stories. Unlike the removed and detached gods and goddesses who weep only for their own losses, the story of Lazarus is an openhearted response to individual suffering that touches us right where we live. Here is the presence of the sacred in our grief—Immanuel—God-with-us.

Like the ancient Chinese goddess Quan Yin, Jesus embodies the qualities of mercy and compassion. The legend says Quan Yin denounced security and a safe haven, returning to the suffering world in order to eternally dispense comfort and mercy. Jesus has also left the safety of another region to answer cries for help. The grieving sisters, the mourners, the perpetually suffering human condition, touch Jesus deeply. A chain of universal human experiences forms a progression from personal pain to shared pain, a progression from detachment to empathy. In our shared grief, we recognize at some deep level that we are all more alike than dissimilar. Along with Jesus and the sisters, and the community of mourners and disciples, we are all invited to move toward the cave where Lazarus is buried.

The action that follows is predicated on an authentic ego-less, internal state of love and empathy springing forth from the enlightened heart. Jesus orders the removal of the stone sealing off the burial cave. It is an odd request. Certainly, if Jesus is able to raise Lazarus from the dead, he is capable of opening the tomb. But here, Jesus is commanding us to get to work. Whatever the major obstacle sealing us into our deadened condition, we need to see that it is removed. Any stuck belief that our situations are hopeless, that nothing can be done, is a kind of fatalism that becomes an impenetrable barrier to life.

Next, Jesus looks up. In looking up, he is directing his attention inward. Like the needle of a compass, he is pointing his consciousness toward the direction of his true source. This is not an external God above us, but the deep reservoir of the Sacred within. Jesus comments he is teaching by showing, and then he expresses gratitude for this connection with his spiritual source. He demonstrates that direct and immediate access to the divine is available anywhere and at any time, even in our deepest sorrow.

Then "Jesus called in a loud voice, 'Lazarus come out.'" This is not meekly begging or supplicating. He is not asking for anything but rather commanding the dead man to leave the tomb and move back into life. "The dead man came out, his hands and feet wrapped with strips of linen and a cloth around his face." What a sight Lazarus must have been as he shuffles out of the tomb still bound in his shroud! "Jesus said to those who were with him, 'Take of the grave clothes and let him go.'" In this final passage, Jesus instructs those who gathered around to help Lazarus remove the trappings of death so he can be free. Jesus models the immanent expression of love in action. He demonstrates caregiving while also empowering others to do the work. He challenges the community to tend to the unclean work that love requires even if it means going beyond our personal boundaries and cultural norms.

This restoration requires the community to give help and offer support. We cannot do this work alone. In our darkest hours, we are unable to move the stone ourselves or lay aside our limiting beliefs, our grave clothes, everything that identifies us as mortally wounded victims. There are times when we are so entrenched in our tombs of deadened spirits we just cannot see a way out. These tasks—the removal of the stone and the grave clothes—are the kinds of gritty actions love demands of us. Lazarus' role in this story is to evoke our compassion. Compassion does its healing work by compelling us to move on, take action, and work together. Through the actions of those who are willing to love, through the gathering of community to tend to the difficult details, through alignment with our spiritual source, and with direct and clear expressed intention, Lazarus experiences rebirth and transformation—from death to life.

REFLECTIONS & QUESTIONS

1. Even in the direst of circumstances, when we have lost all hope, the perseverance of others who care can see us through. We experience this in our own lives and in our national responses to global disasters.
   Have you been a recipient of this kind of care? Have you extended it to others?

2. Jesus instructs the community as to what actions to take to restore Lazarus to life, including:

   - Empathy, a lack of ego
   - Identifying and confronting the obstacles such as habits, beliefs, etc., and seeing to their removal
   - Direct connection with our spiritual source and heartfelt gratitude
   - Clear, expressed intentions; and
   - Working together with others in community to help remove the persona of victimhood and reveal the whole person inside.

   Reflect on these practical instructions and how you might use them to confront the dead places in your life.

Ruth Ann Lonardelli

The Dream That Awakens Us:
Pilate's Wife

When he was accused by the chief priests and the elders, he gave no answer. Then Pilate asked him, "Don't you hear the testimony they are bringing against you?" But Jesus made no reply, not even to a single charge—to the great amazement of the governor.

Now it was the governor's custom at the festival to release a prisoner chosen by the crowd. At that time they had a well-known prisoner whose name was Jesus Barabbas. So when the crowd had gathered, Pilate asked them, "Which one do you want me to release to you: Jesus Barabbas, or Jesus who is called the Messiah?" For he knew it was out of self-interest that they had handed Jesus over to him.

While Pilate was sitting on the judge's seat, his wife sent him this message: "Don't have anything to do with that innocent man, for I have suffered a great deal today in a dream because of him."

But the chief priests and the elders persuaded the crowd to ask for Barabbas and to have Jesus executed.

MATTHEW 27:12-20 (NIV)

THE DREAM AWAKENS HER FROM A DEEP SLEEP AND SHE bolts upright on her bed. She is unaccustomed to arising this early, but she has no desire to risk sleep and another nightmare like this one. Although the details are already dissolving into wispy fragments, it is clear the dream was about the prisoner her husband had taken in yesterday. What a horrible dream! Blood and anguish, such suffering. It all seemed so real. She moves about her room, hoping to shake off the darkness, but the dream's residue sticks, becoming more and more dense, until it feels like a thick fog is enveloping her. She is wide-awake and yet still caught in a miasma of dread. She has just had one of those mystifying dreams from which we wake. Like so many, she lives as if sleepwalking, until something awakens her from the trance of her everyday life.

Prior to the dream of Pilate's wife, the disciples have accompanied Jesus into the Garden of Gethsemane. It is a time of deep foreboding. The lively conversations of just hours before are over. Jesus has gone apart to pray, to seek guidance and comfort. He asks his disciples to hold the watch with him, but as soon as Jesus retreats into prayer the men fall asleep. When he returns, he finds them sleeping. "Could you men not keep watch with me for one hour?"

His words cause the men to stir. They are reminded to stay present, alert, and prayerful, but no sooner does Jesus return to his vigil, than they return to sleep. This incident repeats again and again, until the Roman guards arrive and take Jesus away. Our human tendency to slip into unconsciousness prevails, especially when faced with difficult challenges. Even when we are nudged awake by a higher awareness—the Christ consciousness—like the disciples in the garden, we remain awake only as long as it takes us to fall asleep again.

Jesus is taken prisoner and marched into court to face the charges against him before Pontius Pilate, the Roman governor. Pilate is listening to the case against Jesus and deliberating over what he has heard, when he receives a short, concise, and evocative message of advice from his wife: "Don't have anything to do with that innocent man, for I have suffered a great deal today in a dream because of him." She is the only one who speaks up in an attempt to prevent the violence that lies ahead. In the Eastern Orthodox Church and the Ethiopian Orthodox Church, as well some other early churches, she is known as "Claudia Procula" and considered a saint.

Over the years, she has been deified by some for attempting to save Jesus, and vilified by others, who see her as a meddling woman interfering with God's divine plan. She has inspired poetry and literature, and she has been seen as a representative of the feminine voice and intuitive knowing. The novelist Antoinette May, author of *Pilate's Wife*, wrote, "I was intrigued by this woman who had a dream and tried to change history."[79]

The sleepless woman serves as a spokesperson for all of us who at some time have experienced a troubling and clear insight that awakens us from our slumber and casts a long and deep shadow over our days. Such insights emanating from the twilight temples of our dreams are often difficult to translate into daytime language. The message the dream conveys might just be found in the unsettling jolt that wakes us up.

There is no record of what follows after her warning is delivered. Certainly, her concerns are disregarded.

Pilate does not appear to reprimand her for speaking up or acknowledge her concerns in any way. Perhaps Pilate wants to escape sentencing Jesus to death, but in the end his allegiance is to the material world and upholding the law. His wife, on the other hand, has access to the world of inner awareness and foresight. All we know of this sleepless woman are the poignant words attributed to her, "…for I have suffered a great deal today." We know how it feels when our unheeded revelations overshadow us. The uneasiness of our deep, unheard concerns leads us to a sense of helplessness and hopelessness, and ultimately to our suffering.

The sleepless woman is like Cassandra, the tragic figure from Greek mythology who is cursed with the insight to apprehend future events without the power to prevent their inevitable outcome. She bears the burden of a gift of foresight fated to go unheeded. The voice of intuition, the voice of Sacred Feminine awareness, is silenced. Her story is a timeless one in which the ability to foretell the consequences of violence and domination is disregarded, resulting in untold suffering. Central to all forms of suppression is the refusal to listen. When not heard, when concerns are not acknowledged and respected, figures such as this one sleepless woman fade away, become troubled, diminished, and nameless. She is retained as a remnant to remind us how we, too, can become a wispy, shadow figure when no one listens to our insights and concerns. We need to be aware of how we also suppress and silence our own voices, placing ourselves in the shadows of history. Her memory also serves to remind us that even if it is unlikely our insights will change the course of events, we cannot choose to remain silent. We might be the only ones listening and expressing our inner knowing, yet we can still express our authentic experience. Then, at least, we choose to live with integrity and speak our truth.

REFLECTIONS & QUESTIONS

1. Although we might know it is important to remain conscious and aware, we often distract and numb ourselves in order to avoid responsible action.
   In what ways do you experience wakefulness? How do you become less awake?

2. Even if no one listens, we cannot run the risk of not speaking our truth. Speaking the truth is essential in order to maintain our integrity and lead an authentic life.
   What is your experience with speaking up against common opinions? How did you experience this in your body? How were you received?

3. We have also suppressed and silenced our own voices, placing ourselves in the shadows of history.
   How do you silence yourself? What internal reserves do you need in order to speak up?

Ruth Ann Lonardelli

Forgiveness, Transformation, and Sustaining the Transformed Self: Easter

Then Jesus went with his disciples to a place called Gethsemane, and he said to them, "Sit here while I go over there and pray." He took Peter and the two sons of Zebedee along with him, and he began to be sorrowful and troubled. Then he said to them, "My soul is overwhelmed with sorrow to the point of death. Stay here and keep watch with me.

Going a little further, he fell with his face to the ground and prayed, "My father, if it is possible, may this cup be taken from me. Yet not as I will, but as you will."

Then he returned to his disciples and found them sleeping. "Could you men not keep watch with me for one hour?" he asked Peter. "Watch and pray so that you will not fall into temptation. The spirit is willing but the flesh is weak."

He went away a second time and prayed, "My Father, if it is not possible for this cup to be taken away unless I drink it, may your will be done."

When he came back he again found them sleeping, because their eyes were heavy. So he left them and went away once more and prayed the third time, saying the same thing.

Then he returned to the disciples and said to them, "Are you still sleeping and resting? Look, the hour is near, and the

Son of Man is betrayed into the hands of sinners. Rise, let us go! Here comes my betrayer!"

MATTHEW 26:36-46 (NIV)

"My God, My God, why have you forsaken me?"

MARK 15:34 (NIV)

"Jesus said, "Father forgive them, for they do not know what they are doing."

LUKE 23:34 (NIV)

THIS IS SUCH A HEART-WRENCHING SCENE. THE VIBRANT spiritual teacher who inspired and healed others now finds himself in the worst possible trouble. Jesus, betrayed and tortured, suffers a terrible death.

At the center is the image of the suffering, dying Jesus, which has survived for centuries as a powerful image of vulnerability. This is also our vulnerability, which we must confront. Loss, conflict, illness, and depression expose us to the fundamental truth of our existence: a state of profound vulnerability underlies any illusion of security we might think we have. We tend to experience our vulnerability as a deep shock. Buddhist teacher Pema Chodron succinctly states, "Life has just nailed us."[80] We might be aware that life is challenging, and also harbor a core belief that it will not expect too much of us.

Eckhart Tolle writes, "Most people cannot conceive of any meaning when their life, their world, is being demolished.

And yet, potentially, there is even deeper meaning here.... This is to say, their inner purpose would emerge only as their outer purpose collapsed and the shell of the ego would begin to crack open."[81] The suffering we face might prove to be an initiation, and, as difficult as it is to imagine at the time, the heartbreaks of our lives can serve as catalysts for spiritual transformation. This is the most universal of stories—the transformation mystery from death to life, the sacrifice of life that assures life is ongoing. Within the Jesus story, we find the universal expression of our timeless struggle with suffering, forgiveness, and the inexplicable, resilient, and regenerative nature of life itself.

Jesus contemplates his fate and offers the heartfelt prayer, "If there is any other way, let this pass." His humanness touches us and his prayer gives voice to our deep longing for reprieve from our own acute suffering. Jesus concludes his prayer with acceptance, "Thy will be done." Acceptance, embracing the tiger, happens when we relinquish any idea we can dodge whatever lies before us.

There are other players in this drama of transformation, each reflecting glimpses into our own story. Jesus asks the men to keep watch with him as he prays in the Garden of Gethsemane, but they fall asleep. We recognize our somnambulistic selves in this. We also have difficulty staying awake and present. Rather than confronting our fears, we slip into unconsciousness. Jesus is confronted by the soldiers, who arrest him, and Peter draws his sword, striking out at one of them. Anger, defensiveness, violence are some of the ways we react to what threatens us. Judas represents betrayal. Peter denies any association with Jesus. These characters point to the stark recognition that what we might have counted on for support—friends, education, careers, our charming personas, and even our faith seem to fail us. A state of chaos ensues. Jesus is mocked, ridiculed, and spat upon. We also encounter critical voices, both external and the inner critics that assail and mock us.

On the cross, Jesus' words echo our deepest misgivings, "My God! My God! Why has thou forsaken me?" What a strange and chilling cry. Is Jesus truly forsaken by God? We barely have the courage to ask the question that logically follows. "If Jesus is forsaken by God, what hope is there for me?" In the midst of such horror—the deep, dark hole of despair—existential grief and doubt are an inevitable slide.

The Gospel of Luke shifts the scene radically by offering still another revelation. In the midst of his suffering, Jesus experiences a moment of profound insight. This is his cosmic "Aha!" and it completely transforms what is happening. For all those who tortured and betrayed him, Jesus then offers up the blessing: "Father, forgive them for they know not what they do." Such a surprisingly gentle blessing, the kind a mother might extend to misbehaving children. It stands in stark contrast to the hateful, vitriolic scene of the crucifixion. Jesus demonstrates the most important of all spiritual teachings: incomprehensible compassion and forgiveness. How did Jesus get to such a state of mastery? Traditional teaching stresses that Jesus came into the world fully cognizant of infinite wisdom and knowledge. This belief does not recognize the important developmental, incremental process he so clearly demonstrates and which serves to teach and inspire us.

Jesus' awakening began at his baptism at the River Jordan, when he received the clear call of the Great Mother Heart of God claiming him as her beloved son. In that moment, he realized this voice would inform and transform his spirituality, his values, and his mission. He increasingly moved away from traditional patriarchy and became whole-heartedly committed to an integrated, balanced, realization of the wholeness of God, the integration of immanent and transcendent aspects of the divine. This led him to the deep introspective work of his wilderness adventure, the work of facing his projections and shadows, yet not identifying with either. He learned the lesson of his own prejudices and contracted heart from the Canaanite woman. From her, he began to recognize that the nature of the Great Mother is to challenge the old separation thinking. The territory of the Mother Heart of God knows no bounds. He expanded his understanding of prayer and healing from a Centurion who showed him the power of an active faith.

Over the course of his ministry, Jesus grew into a radiant messenger of Christ consciousness. His practices led him to places in himself of higher awareness and connection with his Sacred Source, which imbued him with wisdom. Then from an inner, centered place, he transitioned seamlessly into tending to the needs of others. He exchanged ego for vulnerability. This breakthrough comes when vulnerability scours us clean of every misguided identification with ego, and even with life itself. In the words of Lao Tze in the Tao Te Ching, "To be whole, let yourself break. To be straight, let yourself bend. To be full, let yourself be empty. To be new, let yourself wear out. To have everything, give everything up."[82] From the deepest suffering, Jesus emerges as the Christ, the Enlightened One, through the power of forgiveness. Jesus reveals that not only is vulnerability inevitable, but as sociologist Brene Brown notes, vulnerability is necessary in order to claim life completely. Our way into and through it is "the birthplace of joy, love, and belonging…."[83] When we recognize and respect the vulnerability of all of life, we realize a common connection that opens our hearts. We come to understand that we are all connected to life by tenuous strands and we need to take care.

The story is commonly told that God, the father, sacrifices Jesus to save humanity from sin. We have been taught to believe this cruel and murderous plot was devised by a loving God for the forgiveness of our sins. This is a troublesome and unfortunate misunderstanding. This story is about forgiveness, yet it is a story about the spiritual transformation springing forth as a deep expression of our soul when we practice forgiveness. Jesus demonstrates, even in the most extreme circumstances, that when we are the most vulnerable, forgiveness offers the possibility of freedom from bitterness and resentment. We are changed when we forgive. Forgiveness is not about forgetting or approving of misdeeds. We recognize the mind's screaming demand for fairness. Forgiveness does not absolve anyone from accountability. But no amount of human justice can ever compensate for acts of violence. Our hearts know this and ache for something more. Rev. Lynden Harris, a priest at St. Paul's Chapel in New York, was at the center of the city's response to the bombing of the World Trade Center on September 11, 2011. In the words of Rev. Harris: "We stand in awe of the horrors that can happen in the world and we decide neither to participate in them nor repay them."[84] When we make the decision that the violence stops with us, we find our heart's deepest longing for peace. We come to make peace with how events unfold while holding the watch for a breakthrough in human consciousness, a time when we no longer consider violence as an option. Our daily prayer becomes, "May this be the day loving-kindness breaks out in the hearts of people everywhere, and we turn to one another and to all species and say, 'Brother! Sister! Friend!'" Jesus is speaking as the Mother Heart of God when he says, "Father, forgive them, for they know not what they do."

Through this radical demonstration, we are shown that forgiveness is not only possible, but this is the work we are called to do. We need to forgive others, and we also need to forgive ourselves. If we do not forgive others, then we are crucified daily with each habitual recollection of the wrong done to us. If we do not forgive ourselves, we are forever nailed to the crosses we bear. Forgiveness is a practice and an ongoing process. Eric Butterworth said, "Forgiveness must be perpetual, a state of consciousness and not just an occasional gesture.... Unforgiveness is a price that man [and women] cannot afford to pay."[85]

Forgiveness creates a healing resonance extending beyond our personal stories to create a pulsation of peace in the hearts of others. Forgiveness work transforms us as we practice, as we forgive and are forgiven. It is a portal into a deepening sense of Sacred Oneness.

Following his revelation that forgiveness is the ultimate triumph, Jesus surrenders. "It is finished." This is the culmination of his life commitment to all he has learned and taught. Surrender to this great truth of forgiveness is the "period at the end of the sentence" that allows for a new story to be written. This surrender is not resignation, but rather stillness, a pause in which events settle down, the senses are quieted, and calmness sets in before we turn to the next page.

Resurrection is the renewed sense of the transformed self. The tomb is now the womb of regeneration. The male disciples have fled. The women are in attendance; they have come to care for the body of Jesus. They serve as midwives for a new life. Mary Magdalene is a demonstration of love, the kind of courageous love that shows up in the face of fear. In all four gospels, Mary Magdalene is named as one of the women consistently present as the events unfold. Cynthia Bouregeault, an Episcopal priest, notes, "When all the other disciples are fleeing, Mary Magdalene stands firm. She does not run; she does not betray or lie about her commitment—she witnesses. Her actions are clearly a demonstration of either the deepest human love or the highest spiritual understanding of what Jesus has been teaching, perhaps both."[86]

Overcome with grief and filled with despair when she finds the tomb empty, Mary does not recognize Jesus, at first. Then he speaks her name, and in that moment Mary recognizes him. It is a powerful and marvelous exchange. Without this moment of recognition and clarity, this naming and claiming of who we are, the miraculous escapes us. An intense spiritual experience can leave us emotionally off balance. Mary's recognition of pure Christ consciousness is her breakthrough awareness, and all her unsettling emotions give way to peace.

Mary is filled with joy and wonder! She returns to tell the disciples about what she has seen, but they do not believe her. Do not expect our insights to be easily understood by others. Others must come to this for themselves and experience their own personal metanoia.

The old theologies offered prescribed ways to transformation. According to those views, we must adopt their laws, beliefs, or professions of faith in order to achieve the benefits of salvation. This is the worst kind of hubris. It is rather like trying to impose man-made laws on the stages of gestation and childbirth. The nature of the process itself moves us along and reveals its full meaning for us in a profoundly personal way. The spiritual consciousness of the Divine Feminine midwifes radical transformation by showing up in love and support, reminding us nothing can separate us from the regenerative love of the Christ.

Sustaining deep change becomes the work of the community. Each one of Jesus' followers has her or his own unique experience. They also gather together to support and inspire one another and share their awakenings. The work of community is crucial and complex. Community performs an important role when it understands and affirms that spiritual transformation is of value. The healthy support of others also helps us return to life and work in a way that keeps us grounded and centered. Community provides us with ample opportunities to practice Jesus' profound teaching of forgiveness and to truly honor its deep work in our lives. Most importantly, community is the keeper of the stories of transformation. Community helps us remember.

REFLECTIONS & QUESTIONS

1. The Easter story comes from a tradition of ancient transformation mysteries—the sacrifice of life, which assures life.
   How does thinking about the Easter story as being an expression of an enduring theme in human consciousness affect its meaning for you? Does its meaning expand or diminish?

2. Vulnerability is necessary in order to claim life completely.
   Reflect on your reaction to this statement.
   Jesus acknowledges what is before him and asks if there is any other way. Then he moves into acceptance. Acknowledgement and acceptance are first steps toward healing.
   Consider the differences between acknowledgement and denial; between acceptance and resignation.

3. Unconsciousness, anger, betrayal, defensiveness, violence, chaos, fear, and grief are some of the many states we experience when we are the most vulnerable.
   How does recognizing these states as a response to vulnerability affect your experience of them?

4. If we do not forgive others, then we are crucified daily with each habitual recollection of the wrong done to us. If we do not forgive ourselves, we are forever nailed to the crosses we bear.
   What does forgiveness mean to you?

5. Once we experience spiritual renewal, the support
   of others helps us sustain our new growth. When
   others love, recognize, and acknowledge us, they
   help us remember we are in new territory. This is
   the kind of support we need to go forward.
   *How have you benefited from the support of
   community? In what ways is community beneficial
   in sustaining your growth? What are the limits of
   community for you?*

Woman, Why Are You Weeping?: Resurrection

On the first day of the week, very early in the morning, the women took the spices they had prepared and went to the tomb. They found the stone rolled away from the tomb, but when they entered, they did not find the body of the Lord Jesus. While they were wondering about this, suddenly two men in clothes that gleamed like lightning stood beside them. In their fright the women bowed down with their faces to the ground, but the men said to them, "Why do you look for the living among the dead? He is not here; he has risen! Remember how he told you, while he was still with you in Galilee: 'The Son of Man must be delivered over to the hands of sinners, be crucified and on the third day be raised again.'" Then they remembered his words.

When they came back from the tomb, they told all these things to the Eleven and to all the others. It was Mary Magdalene, Joanna, Mary the mother of James, and the others with them who told this to the apostles. But they did not believe the women, because their words seemed to them like nonsense. Peter, however, got up and ran to the tomb. Bending over, he saw the strips of linen lying by themselves, and he went away, wondering to himself what had happened.

LUKE 24:1-12 (NIV)

Ruth Ann Lonardelli

He asked her, "Woman, why are you crying? Who is it you are looking for?"

Thinking he was the gardener, she said, "Sir, if you have carried him away, tell me where you have put him, and I will get him."

Jesus said to her, "Mary."

She turned toward him and cried out in Aramaic, "Rabboni!" (which means "Teacher").

Jesus said, "Do not hold on to me, for I have not yet ascended to the Father. Go instead to my brothers and tell them, 'I am ascending to my Father and your Father, to my God and your God.'"

Mary Magdalene went to the disciples with the news: "I have seen the Lord!" And she told them that he had said these things to her.

JOHN 20: 15-18 (NIV)

THE WOMEN GATHER AT THE SCENE OF THE HORROR—Mary, his mother, Salome, his sister, Mary Magdalene, and in one version, Joanna, another of the disciples. Other women stand just beyond on a hillside overlook. A bold, golden sun lights up the sky. Ash-colored birds glide toward the horizon. The women pull up their scarves attempting to block out the putrid smells. The gesture is of little use. They can neither muffle the awful moaning and cries of those still alive nor avert their sight from the dazed and glassy stares—the spattering of blood everywhere, the dying and dead. They witness it all while their attention is focused on the one whom they love. He is hanging on the cross. Their throats are raw from weeping, and their fear is so taut it holds them upright despite the drift they feel in their bones. They feel all of the grief, confusion, and fear, and yet they remain present. Most of the men have fled. The women serve as witnesses, attendants, the ones whose bonds of love and friendship persevere through fear and grief.

There is a version of this story in each of the gospels. Much like in the beginning, when Mary, the mother of Jesus, and Elizabeth gave birth to a new spirituality, the story at the end of Jesus' life is also told within the context of a community of women. Here they hold vigil, offer support, recognize, acknowledge, and then attempt to share the mystery of transformation. Once again the absence of the masculine indicates this is an activity of the heart, because our rational minds cannot truly comprehend this mystery. Here, mystical revelations and spiritual endurance unfold from the shared experience of the women.

Jesus' body is removed to the tomb for burial. The women follow. They gather at the tomb holding vigil. Stunned and confused, they murmur their sorrow and weep their despair.

The hours wear on. The women grieve together. Because of Jewish cleanliness laws around caring for the dead, they cannot anoint Jesus' body for burial until after the Sabbath. The sharing of grief turns to planning how to carefully tend to Jesus' burial. This is an intricate web of relationships. One woman knows where to find the freshest spices; another, the source for the most precious cloth. Each one has her task to do. The work arises spontaneously as they collaborate and focus on their intention to lovingly attend to the broken body of their beloved teacher. Some leave to collect the things they will need. Others remain behind to hold vigil.

Somehow in the midst of their inner turmoil, they have the presence of mind to take care of all these details.

In the early dawn hours of the following day, a group of women gathers and begins their return to the burial caves. The gauzy, lavender sky muffles the soft sounds of morning. A morning cook fire crackles, shooting sparks into the air. A donkey brays. A lone bird sings in an olive tree. Other small jittery birds scratch up puffs of dust from the hard soil. The women murmur to one another, carefully cradling the vessels of precious ointments in their arms. The scent of pungent spices fills the morning air: the heavy, rich fragrance of myrrh, the sweet piercing smell of the frankincense, the soft and fresh sandalwood.

You can hear the subdued whispers of the women and the creak of their scandals as they shift their weight. There seems no end to their tears. They begin to share their thoughts. They are afraid. They are worried. Who will roll away the stone from the tomb? The stone is large and too heavy for them to remove. No men are available to help them. This part of the story is sometimes told in a way that ridicules the women's fears. Seldom has their courage and willingness been acknowledged. There is little mention that the men were too frightened to show up at all. These women worry about how they will get it all done and yet they take the next steps anyway. They have concerns, but they do not let their concerns stop them. This is the worry that walks.

In the Christianity that developed long after Jesus lived and died, the central theology focused on the transcendent aspect of the divine. This serves a purpose in orienting us to a larger story than our own; however, a singular focus on the transcendent translates into a hierarchal system that denies life. Our earthly experience and expression of life becomes profane. Such a hierarchal spiritual concept of the sacred comes at a cost. Many church fathers viewed life and all its messy emotional content with suspicion and considered feeling states a distraction from the more acceptable contemplative practices. Expressions of raw grief, worry, and even joy tended to be moderated or suppressed. The God of Transcendence was above all these untidy annoyances. Ecstatic emotional expressions of the heart were generally associated with mysticism, which was largely the domain of women. Mystics were most often silenced and condemned. According to this widely held view, head and heart are uneasy companions. Such a bias does not bode well for the integration of the sacred immanence and sacred transcendent aspects of the divine. Andrew Harvey writes, "The addiction to transcendence keeps everybody in a coma, tells you your emotions are too much, your desires are absurd and obscene, your passions for justice are naïve. This addiction…keeps you self-absorbed and falsely detached…."[87]

When the rational mind takes precedence over the heart, we sacrifice intuitive wisdom to the mind's exclusive claim of sacred knowledge and expression. We trade life-affirming passion, relational spirituality, and a sense of our place in the earth family for domination and alienation. Rather than disregard the sacred insights of our pure authentic feelings, the mystic Rumi, in the poem, *The Guest House*, teaches us that feelings are transient visitors who come and go. When we understand how this works, how our emotions neither dim the divine spark within us nor do they define us, we can be at peace with our humanness. Rumi makes the point that we should acknowledge our feeling states as temporary visitors and understand their nature is to move on. We might entertain emotions, but we are also more than our emotions. Rumi says treat them as honored guests because feelings can be spiritually revealing:

The Guest House

This being human is a guest house.
Every morning a new arrival.

A joy, a depression, a meanness,
some momentary awareness comes
as an unexpected visitor.

Welcome and entertain them all!
Even if they're a crowd of sorrows,
who violently sweep your house
empty of its furniture,
still, treat each guest honorably.
He may be clearing you out
for some new delight.

The dark thought, the shame, the malice,
meet them at the door laughing, and invite them in.
Be grateful for whoever comes,
because each has been sent
as a guide from beyond.[88]

The women's complex emotional concerns of worry and grief stir up their core energies. They are compelled to action, to serve and follow their vision to completion. The women arrive at the tomb and find it opened. They reach for each other, move together toward the entrance of the cave to look inside. They are met by two luminous beings informing them Jesus is not there. In one version, an angel asks Mary Magdalene, "Why do you seek the living among the dead?" This deeply evocative spiritual question challenges her to expand her awareness. The angel is asking Mary, "How can you expect to regenerate new life from old patterns and worn-out beliefs?" This is not a reproach, but a meaningful question in the service of spiritual awakening. Mary Magdalene's traditional beliefs, and even the radical ways her beliefs have shifted and expanded in recent months, no longer serve her. In her spiritual journey, Mary is not just exchanging an old religion for a newer one. All of the seeking is over, done with, dead! She is experiencing an even more expansive, selfless experience into the wholeness of God where nothing is missing.

Mary Magdalene sees the empty tomb, and she is lured by the seduction of human thoughts to fall deeper into despair. The story she starts to spin speaks to our common inclination to create stories from our fears and imaginations. She begins to think someone has taken away the body of Jesus and hidden him. She might not ever be able to find him.

Then Mary turns around. Like the turning of Sufi dervishes, this turning is toward the mystical awareness of the divine. A shift is about to occur; another perspective about to be revealed. Standing before her, someone she takes to be a gardener asks her, "Woman, why are you weeping?" This question addresses the universal sorrow of broken-hearted people everywhere. This gentle inquiry is an empathetic expression of the heart and an acknowledgement of what Mary is experiencing. Grief and sadness are met and held with compassion. She answers him, telling him about her concerns, her grief and longing. This voicing of what is deeply felt—and its being wholeheartedly received—is radically compassionate and profoundly healing. Speaking our grief and being genuinely heard, without distracting commentary, clears our emotional energy and allows deep insight and peace to emerge.

Then Jesus, as the fully realized Christ, says to her, "Mary." At this point, she is called to a radical new awareness. She is called away from the deep grief of the separate self into the liberation of sacred unity. Mary is called to wholeness and she answers the call. She turns around again, turning away from her spotlight attention, focused on what has been lost, and she sees the enduring floodlight radiance of the Beloved.

At the center of the cross, we realize a transformative connection, union, integration, and the annihilation of duality. Transcendence—symbolized by the vertical line of the cross, the grand upsweep of Father God—offers release from earthly suffering. Immanence—symbolized by the horizontal line of the cross—represents life itself and the Great Compassionate Mother God. This is the expression of love and connection we experience in our ordinary lies. At the cross, these two aspects of the divine meet at the center, and the union of transcendence and immanence explodes into the infinite, shattering the surface sense of existence, ripping open the veil between the world of form and the infinity of spirit, revealing the pulsating, emanating heart of the divine. Only this infinite moment of sacred oneness exists. The yearning of the transcendent and the immanent for each other, for full expression, is realized in this encounter of Mary Magdalene and the Christ. Everything Mary seeks has already been found. She is ecstatic! Joyful! The power of love that radiates in Mary as the feminine principle of the soul empowers her through all the confusion, doubt, fear, and worry. She has moved through the circuit of her human concerns and entered into the mystery of metanoia, a state of profound spiritual transformation. Jesus as Christ has shattered the illusion of the separate self and revealed the ever-unfolding, expansive Now. Not only has death's mystique as the final word been broken, restoration is surpassed and becomes eternal radiance. This transformative mystery is the work of the Sacred Feminine. "Transformation," says author and teacher Joan Chamberlain Engelsman, "is only possible when what is to be transformed enters wholly into the Feminine Principle of dying and return."[89] This surrendering to the wisdom of Mother God allows the old ways to be crushed and broken, while trusting in the resilience and regeneration of life itself.

Along with deep transformation comes the irrepressible, passionate yearning of the soul to share this mystery with others. Mary runs to tell the men, the disciples, of her experience, her insight, and her inspiration. It is now a beautiful spring morning, bright and clear. The scent of spring flowers, of Earth's spices, fills the air. Mary's heart is pounding with excitement. She runs, glides really, angel-footed, and arrives breathless, spilling out her story from the depths of her soul. But they do not believe her. This is the challenge of the transformative mystery—it is incomprehensible to the rational mind.

Authors Cynthia Avens and Richard Zelley write, "In the Gospel of John it is Mary Magdalene who provides the 'model of discipleship' rather than Peter. It is Mary Magdalene who bravely stays at the cross during the crucifixion, who is the first to witness the risen Christ, and who is told to carry the message of Christ's resurrection to the other disciples...."[90] Through the revisionist patriarchy of the church, Mary Magdalene was fashioned into a reformed prostitute, which is "…a tragic distortion of the character presented…as the most faithful disciple who is the first to truly understand the full meaning of Christ's revelation." Mary Magdalene might have received the divine vision personally, but she did not walk through her experience alone. She went in the company of other women. In contrast to the hero's solitary journey and the high value we place on rugged individualism, this is the way of women: to go together through the experience of life. Just as in the beginning when Jesus' mother, Mary, and Elizabeth shared their creative gifts and mutual support in birthing the sacred, these women at the end of the story come together to grieve and attend to the details of the burial, to validate and affirm their deep experience.

Recent scientific studies provide some insight about the biological basis for all this togetherness. A study from ULCA concludes, "When the hormone oxytocin (the cuddle hormone) is released as part of the stress response in a woman, it buffers the 'fight or flight' response and encourages her to tend children and gather with other women instead. When she actually engages in this tending or befriending, studies suggest more oxytocin is released, which further counters stress and produces a calming effect. According to Dr. Klein, "This calming response does not occur in men, because testosterone—which men produce in high levels when they're under stress—seems to reduce the effects of oxytocin. Estrogen seems to enhance it."[91] Tending and befriending are activities of compassion and expressions of the Immanent Sacred Feminine aspect of the divine.

Unlike many religious practices which distance us from life, the Sacred Feminine is always calling us back to ourselves. Every moment is sacred here, every mundane action and reaction is a potential expression of devotion. The phone call to a troubled friend, feeding our children and families, and caring for animals, these actions become sacraments that teach us patience in the messy business of life and love. The Sacred Feminine refuses to cast us adrift from our ordinary lives and the sanctity of the interconnected web of life. In the pre-Christian Jesus stories, the values of the Sacred Feminine are threaded together like precious jewels onto the strand of the Christ. They shine with a brilliant light, exposing the patriarchal notion of separation for the deception it is. They awaken us to the expanded understanding that home and belonging are not to be found elsewhere, outside of ourselves. They are right where we are. Our spiritual practice lies in the care we extend to one another and to the planet—our precious, irreplaceable home. Our response to the world's needs and the ecological destruction around us must be to show up as the women did in this story. We must persevere through our worries and concerns, and serve as witnesses. We must lovingly tend to the destruction around us with our gifts, and, like Mary Magdalene, let our passionate longing for the sacred be so all-consuming that it shatters our fears and concerns, our obsolete faith, and our limited ideas about what love is. Then we will be compelled to see the wholeness beyond duality, beyond male and female, beyond life and death. In this way, we will experience a breakthrough into floodlight consciousness, to a boundless connection with radiant oneness—Alaha, Sacred Unity, our true Christ, our own true Buddha nature.

REFLECTIONS & QUESTIONS

1. Mary is asked two very provocative questions, "Why do you seek the living among the dead?" This is not a reproach, but a question that stimulates deep reflection and assists Mary in turning toward a new direction rather than holding on to what she has always known.
   How would you have responded to the angel's question to Mary? In what ways does resorting to patterns and solutions from the past limit you in your personal and spiritual growth?

2. The second question asked of Mary is, "Woman, why are you weeping?"
   How is the acknowledgement of your experiences an empathetic expression of the heart? How does this shift what you are experiencing?

3. Working through our difficulties together with others is sometimes seen as antithetical to a "heroic" process of going it alone.
   How has this cultural bias affected the way you deal with life's challenges?

4. Mary turns from a spotlight consciousness to floodlight consciousness, from grief to radiance.
   How would you describe your experience with these two states of consciousness? Can you recognize these states as you experience them? How can the recognition of what precipitates each, help us in the way we experience them?

ACKNOWLEDGEMENTS

It is with the deepest appreciation and gratitude that I acknowledge the work of so many diligent researchers, talented authors, and inspired teachers who have helped shape the ideas in this book. They are listed in the notes and bibliography that follow, and it is my earnest recommendation that readers avail themselves of these fine works in their entirety.

My deepest appreciation for the staff at Luminare Press, Patricia Marshall, Kim Harper-Kennedy and Claire Flint Last, for their patience and remarkable talents. My heartfelt thanks for all the loving support and insightful feedback from Mary Inn Burdette and Lois Caswell, and, of course, my sister, Nancy. And, for my beloved husband, Richard, who listened so intently even as he leaned into the mystery of his last precious years – my boundless gratitude for showing me there is more love here than we can possibly imagine.

ABOUT THE AUTHOR

Ruth Ann (Annie) Lonardelli, M.A. is an ordained Interfaith minister, teacher, spiritual mentor, and author. She served as co-founder and spiritual leader at Unity Center Of Peace in Bothell, Washington. Annie leads workshops, classes and retreats and is a popular guest speaker in churches and other organizations. She lives in the Pacific Northwest.

BIBLIOGRAPHY

Armstrong, Karen. *The Bible*. New York: Atlantic Monthly Press, 2007.

_____. *A History of God*. New York: Ballantine Books, 1993.

Arnold, Rev. Talitha. "Gifts from the Desert." *Reflections - Women's Journeys: Progress and Peril*, vol. 98, #1, Yale Divinity School, Spring 2011.

Artress, Lauren. *The Sacred Path Companion: A Guide to Walking the Labyrith to Heal and Transform*. New York: Riverhead Books, 2006.

Avens, Cynthia & Zelley Richard. *Walking the Path of Christo-Sophia – Exploring the hidden Tradition in Christian Spirituality*. Bloomington, Indiana: Author House, 2005.

Bauckham, Richard. *Gospel Women – Studies of the Named Women in the Gospels*. Grand Rapids, Michigan: Eerdmans Publishing Co., 2002.

Boehm, Toni. *Embracing the Feminine Nature of the Divine*. Greenwood, MO: Inner Visioning Press, 2001.

Borg, Marcus J. & John Dominic Crossan, *The First Paul – Reclaiming the Radical Visionary Behind the Church's Conserative Icon*. New York: Harper One, 2009.

Borysenko, Joan. *A Woman's Journey to God*. New York: Riverhead Books, 1999.

Bouregeault, Cynthia. *The Meaning of Mary Magdalene – Discovering the Woman at the Heart of Christianity.* Boston & London: Shambhala, 2010.

Brown, Brene. TED talk http://www.youtube.com/watch?v=X4Qm9cGRub0.

Burgo, Joseph. "Basic Shame, Toxic Shame." online article, http://www.afterpsychotherapy.com/basic-shame/?more=all, 2011.

Butterworth, Eric. *Discover the Power Within You: A Guide to Unexplored Depths Within.* New York: Harper Collins, 1989.

Campbell, Joseph. *The Power of Myth - with Bill Moyers,* Ed. Betty Sue Flowers. New York: Doubleday, 1991.

Chodron, Pema. *When Things Fall Apart, Heart Advice for Difficult Times.* Boston: Shambhala, 1997.

Crossan, John Dominic & Jonathan L. Reed. *Excavating Jesus – Beneath the Stones, Behind the Texts.* San Francisco: Harper Collins, 2001.

Dart, John. "Balancing Out the Trinity: The Genders of the Godhead." *Christian Century.* Christian Century Foundation. February 16-23, 1983.

Douglas-Klotz, Neil. *Prayers of the Cosmos – Meditations on the Aramaic Words of Jesus.* San Francisco: Harper, 1990.

_____. *Decoding the Spiritual Message of the Aramaic Jesus.* Wheaton, Il.: Quest Books, 1999.

Ehrman, Bart D. *Lost Christianities – The Battles for Scripture and the Faiths We Never Knew.* Oxford/New York: Oxford University Press, 2003.

_____. *Jesus Interrupted – Revealing the Hidden Contradictions in the Bible (and Why We Don't Know About*

Them). New York: Harper One, 2009.

_____. *Misquoting Jesus – The Story Behind Who Changed the Bible and Why.* San Francisco: Harper, 2007.

Eisler, Rianne. *The Chalice and The Blade, Our History, Our Future.* New York: Harper Collins, 1988.

Elias, Jack. *Finding True Magic – A Radical Synthesis of Eastern & Western Perspectives & Techniques.* Seattle: Five Wisdom Publications, 1999.

Ellens, Helen &. Wayne G. Rollins. *Psychology and the Bible From Gospel to Gnostics. A New Way to Read Scriptures. vol 3. Westport, Connecticut:* Greenwood Publishing Group, 2004.

Emmons, Robert A. *Thanks! How Practicing Gratitude Can Make You Happier.* Boston/New York: Houghton Mifflin Company, 2008.

Falcon, Ted, Don MacKenzie, & Jamal Rahman. *Getting to the Heart of Interfaith – The Eye-Opening, Hope-Filled Friendship of a Pastor, a Rabbi & a Sheikh.* Woodstock, Vermont: Skylight Paths Publishing, 2010.

Fillmore, Charles. *Teach Us to Pray.* Kansas City, MO: Unity School, 1941. Republished by Forgotten Books, 2008.

Foley, Helene, P. *The Homeric Hymn to Demeter.* New Jersey: University of Princeton Press, 1991.

Freke, Timothy & Peter Gandy. *Jesus and the Lost Goddess – The Secret Teachings of the Original Christians.* New York: Three Rivers Press, 2001.

Funk, Robert W. & Mahlon H. Smith. *The Gospel of Mark – Red Letter Edition.* Sonoma, California: Polebridge Press, 1991.

Funk, Robert T. & The Jesus Seminar, *The Acts of Jesus –*

What did Jesus Really Do? The Search for the Authentic Deeds of Jesus. San Francisco: Harper, 1998.

Funk, Robert W. Roy W Hoover & The Jesus Seminar. *The Five Gospels – What Did Jesus Really Say? The Search for the Authentic Words of Jesus.* San Francisco: Harper, 1997.

Gibran, Kahlil. "The Song of the Song," *The Treasured Writings of Kahlil Gibran.* Ed. Andrew Dib Serfan, Garden City, N.J.: Philosophical Library, Inc. 1965.

Gilligan, Carol. *In A Different Voice: Psychologist Theory and Women's Development.* Cambridge: Harvard, 1982.

Gimbutas, Marija. *The Goddesses and Gods of Old Europe - Myths and Cult Images.* Berkeley and Los Angeles: University of California Press, 1982.

Goldsmith, Joel S. *The Altitude of Prayer.* Athens, GA.: Acropolis Books, 1975.

Guruge, Ananda W.P. "The Buddha's Encounters with Mara the Tempter – Their Representation in Literature and Art." Online article. http://www.accesstoinsight.org/lib/authors/guruge/wheel419.html

Hafiz. *The Gift, Poems by Hafiz.* Trans. Daniel Ladinsky. New York: Penguin Compass, 1999.

_____. *The Subject Tonight is Love, 60 Wild and Sweet Poems of Hafiz.* Trans. Daniel Ladinsky. New York: Penguin Compass, 1996.

Hanh, The Venerable Thich Nhat. *Creating True Peace – Ending the Violence in Yourself, Your Family, Your Community and The World.* New York: Free Press, 2003.

Hall, Nor. *The Moon and the Virgin.* New York: Perennial, 1994. Harpur, Tom. *The Pagan Christ – Is Blind Faith Killing Christianity?* New York: Walker Publishing Co., 2004.

Hart, Hilary. *The Unknown She – Eight Faces of an Emerging Consciousness.* Inverness, CA.: The Golden Sufi Center, 2003.

Harvey, Andrew. *The Divine Feminine, Exploring the Feminine Face of God Around the World.* Berkeley, CA.: Conari Press, 1996.

Harvey, Andrew. *The Return of The Mother.* Berkeley, CA.: Frog, Ltd., 1995.

Heron, John. "Relational Spirituality." P2P Foundation. Online Article, http://p2pfoundation.et/Relational_Spirituality.

H.H. Dalai Lama. *For the Benefit of All Beings: A Commentary on the Way of the Bodhisattva.* Trans. by Padmakara Group. Boston, Shambhala Classics, 2006.

Hughes, Langston. *Selected Poems of Langston Hughes.* New York: Random House, Vintage Edition, 1990.

Johnson, Will. *The Spiritual Practice of Rumi, Radical Techniques for Beholding the Divine.* Rochester, Vermont: Inner Traditions, 2007.

King, Karen. *The Gospel of Mary Magdala: Jesus and the First Woman Apostle.* Santa Rosa, CA.: Polebridge Press, 2003.

May, Antoinette. *Pilate's Wife – A Novel of the Roman Empire.* New York: Harper, 2007.

McTaggart, Lynne. *The Bond – Connecting Through the Space Between Us.* New York: Free Press, 2011.

Meyers, Carol. *Women in Scripture. A Dictionary of Named and Unnamed Women in the Hebrew Bible, The Apocryphal/Deuterocanonical Books, and the New Testament.* Assoc. Eds. Craven & Kraemer. Boston/NewYork:

Houghton Mifflin, 2000.

Moon, Susan. "Grandmother Mind." Shambhala Sun, September 2007.

Newmann, Erich. *The Great Mother – An Analysis of the Archetype.* Princeton, N.J.: Bollingen Series, Princeton University Press, 1974.

Rahman, Jamal. *The Fragrance of Faith – The Enlightened Heart of Islam.* Bath, England: The Book Foundation, 2004.

Ravindra, Ravi. *The Gospel of John in the Light of Indian Mysticism.* Rochester, Vermont: Inner Traditions, 2004.

Rosenberg, Marshall. *Speak Peace in a World of Conflict.* Encinitas, CA.: Puddle Dancer Press, 2005.

Ruether, Rosemary Radford. *Sexism and God-Talk, Toward a Feminist Theology.* Boston: Beacon Press, 1993.

_____. *Women and Redemption, A Theological History.* Minneapolis: Fortress Press, 1998.

Rumi, Jelahuddin. "Let The Lover Be Disgraceful." *Selected Poems.* Trans. Coleman Barks. New York: Penguin, 2004.

_____. "The Guest House." *Essential Rumi.* Trans. Coleman Barks. San Francisco: Harper, 1995.

_____. *Rumi: The Book of Love: Poems of Ecstasy and Longing,* Trans. Coleman Barks. New York: Harper Collins, 2003.

_____. *The Illuminated Rumi.* Trans. Coleman Barks, Illustrator, Michael Green. New York: Bantam, Doubleday, 1997.

Sabin, Marie. *Reopening the Word: Reading Mark as Theology in the Context of Early Judaism.* New York: Oxford University Press, 2002.

Salzberg, Sharon. *Faith – Trusting Your Own Deepest Experience*. New York: Riverhead Books, 2002.

Sanford, John A. *Mystical Christianity – A Psychological Commentary on the Gospel of John*. New York: Crossroads Publishing Co., 1995.

_____. *The Kingdom Within – The Inner Meaning of Jesus' Sayings*. San Francisco: Harper, 1970.

Schmidt, Alvin. *How Christianity Changed the World*. Originally published under the title *Under the Influence: How Christianity Transformed Civilization*. Grand Rapids: Zondervan, 2001.

Shantideva. *The Way of the Bodhisattva: A Translation of the Bodhicharyavatara*. Boston: Shambhala, 1997.

Sheldrake, Philip. *The New Westminister Dictionary of Christian Spirituality*. Louisville, KY.: John Knox Press, First American Edition, 2005.

Silverman, David P. *Ancient Egypt*. New York: Oxford University Press, 2003.

Simic, Vesela. "The Challenge of Forgiveness." *Shift: At the Frontiers of Consciousness*. No. 13 (Dec. 2006-Feb. 2007).

Sjoo, Monica & Barbara Mor. *The Great Cosmic Mother – Rediscovering the Religion of the Earth*. San Francisco: Harper, 1991.

Sopa, Geshe Lhundba. *Steps on the Path to Enlightenment*. Ed. David Patt. Ithaca, New York: Snow Lion Press, 2000.

Spong, John Shelby. *Jesus For The Non Religious*. San Francisco: Harper, 2007.

_____. *Return of the Feminine and the World Soul*. Inverness, CA.: The Golden Sufi Center, 2009.

_____.*The Sins of Scripture, Exposing the Bible's Texts of Hate to Reveal the God of Love.* San Francisco: Harper, 2005.

Stone, Merlin. *When God Was A Woman.* New York: Harcourt Brace Jovanovich, 1976.

Suzuki, Shunryu.., *50 Spiritual Classics: Timeless Wisdom from 50 Great Books of Inner Discovery, Enlightenment & Purpose.* Ed. Tom Butler-Bowdon. London/Boston: Nicholas Brealey Publishing, 2005.

Swimme, Brian. "Awakening to the Universe Story." Online article. http://www.enlightennext.org/magazine/j34/swimme1.asp?page=3/.

Teasdale, Wayne. *The Mystic Heart – Discovering A Universal Spirituality in the World's Religions.* Novato, CA.: New World Library, 2001.

Tolle, Eckhart. *A New Earth: Awakening to Your Life's Purpose.* New York: Penguin, 2005.

Tzu, Lao. *Tao Te Ching.* Ed. George Crank. www.bergen.edu/faculty/gcronk/ TTC.html. 1999.

Vaughan-Lee, Llewellyn. "Inner Work." The Omega Institute for Holistic Studies, www.youtube.com interview, March 23, 2007.

Varner, Gary R. *Water from the Sacred Well - Further Explorations in the Folklore and Mythology of Sacred Waters.* Raleigh, N.C.: OakChylde Books, 2010.

Walker, Barbara G. *Man Made God.* Seattle: Stellar House Publishing, 2010.

Watts, Alan. *The Tao of Philosophy, The Edited Transcripts.* Boston: Tuttle Publishing, 1995.

Wiesel, Elie & Marion. *Night.* New York: Hill & Wang of

Farrar, Straus & Giroux, 1985.

Wheatley, Margaret J. *Finding Our Way – Leadership for an Uncertain Time.* San Francisco: Berrett-Koehler, 2005.

Wilber, Ken. "Introduction to Integral Theory and Practice, IOS Practice and the AQAL Map." Online *Journal of Integral Theory and Practice, Spring 2006, vol #1* http://aqaljournal.integralinstitute.org/Pdf/Vol1_No1_Final_02_11_07_opt.pdf.

Wilson, Martin. *In Praise of Tara: Songs of the Saviouress.* Boston: Wisdom Publications, 1986/1996.

The New Schaff-Herzog Encyclopedia of Religious Knowledge. Baker Book House, 1960.

The Encyclopedia of Religion. vol. 2, McMillan, 1987.

The Jewish Encyclopedia. KTAV Pub. House Inc. vol. II.

Holy Bible – New International Version. Zondervan Publishing House: Grand Rapids, Michigan.

ENDNOTES

1. Barbara G. Walker, *Man Made God* (Seattle: Stellar House, 2010), p. 210.

2. Karen Armstrong, *The Bible*, chapter 3, "The Gospel," pp. 55-78.

3. Joseph Campbell, *The Power of Myth*. The theme of spiritual significance in myths recurs throughout many of Campbell's written works. Various references to this were also made in his lectures, notably Seattle and Portland, Jungian Society lectures in the 1980s.

4. Karen Armstrong, *The Bible*, chapter 4, "Midrash," pp. 79-101.

5. John Dominic Crossan, *Pagan Christ*, "Who is Jesus," p. 1.

6. Iman Jamal Rahman, *Getting to the Heart of Interfaith, The Eye-Opening, Hope Filled Friendship of a Pastor, a Rabbit and a Sheikh*, p. 18.

7. Tom Harpur, *Pagan Christ*, pp.4-5.

8. Bart Ehrman, *Lost Christianities*, p. 1.

9. Bart Ehrman, *Jesus Interrupted*, p. 215

10. Bart Ehrman, Lost Christianities, p. 195.

11. Ibid, p. 219

12. John Heron, "Relational Spirituality," P2P Foundation, http://p2pfoundation.et/Relational_Spirituality.

13. Alan Watts, *The Tao of Philosophy, The Edited Transcripts*, pp. 11-12.

14. Richard Bauckham, *Gospel Women – Studies of the Named Women in the Gospels*, pp. 117, 187.

15. Karen King, *The Gospel of Mary Magdala: Jesus and the First Woman Apostle*, p.3.

16. Bart Ehrman, *Jesus Interrupted*, p. 195.

17. Riane Eisler, *The Chalice and The Blade*, p. 21.

18. Ibid. p. 24.

19. Merlin Stone, *When God Was A Woman*, p. 130.

20. Riane Eisler, *The Chalice and The Blade*, p. 48.

21. Ibid, p. xvii.

22. Bart Ehrman, *Lost Christianities,* p. 46.

23. Barbara G. Walker, *Man Made God*, p. 201.

24. John Shelby Spong, *Sins of the Scripture*, p. 97.

25. Andrew Harvey, in the introduction, *Embracing the Feminine Nature of the Divine* by Tony Boehm, pg. ix.

26. T. S. Elliot, "Four Quartets," *The Norton Anthology of Poetry*, p. 1014.

27. Charles Fillmore, talk given in 1916.

28. Ken Wilber, summarizing the findings of Carol Gilligan in his article, "Introduction to Integral Theory and Practice, IOS Practice and

the AQAL Map," *Journal of Integral Theory and Practice*, Spring 2006, Vol #1 online http://aqaljournal.integralinstitute.org/Pdf/Vol1_No1_Final_02_11_07 _opt.pdf.

29. Barbara G. Walker, *Man Made God*, p. 70.

30. Brian Swimme, "Awakening to the Universe Story," http://www.enlightennext.org/magazine/j34/swimme1.asp?page=3/

31. Riane Eisler, *The Chalice and The Blade*, p. 120.

32. Karen Armstong, *The History of God*, pp. 23-25.

33. Sukuki Roshi, "The Second Jewel: The Dharma," by Arnie Kozak, Ph.D. http://www.netplaces.com/buddhism/.

34. McTaggart, Lynne. *The Bond – Connecting Through the Space Between Us*, p. 154.

35. *The Gospel of Thomas*, saying 113.

36. Hafiz, "It Felt Love," *The Gift, Poems of Hafiz*, translations by Daniel Ladinsky, p. 121.

37. Lynne McTaggart, *The Bond – Connecting Through the Space Between Us*, p. xxi.

38. Ibid, p. xxvi.

39. Charles Fillmore as quoted in *Embracing the Feminine Nature of the Divine, Integrative Spirituality Heralds the Next Phase of Conscious Evolution* by Toni Boehm, p. 49.

40. Meister Eckhart (1260-1328, German Dominican monk) as quoted in "Christianity" (1995) by Joe Jenkins, p. 27.

41. Joseph Campbell, *The Power of Myth - with Bill Moyers*, p. 209-210.

42. Kahlil Gibran, "The Song of the Song," *The Treasured Writings of Kahlil Gibran*, ed. Andrew Dib Serfan, p. 42.

43. Eihei Dogen, Zen master, founder of the Soto School. From the article,"Grandmother Mind," by Susan Moon online, *Shambhala Sun*. http://www.shambhalasun.com/index.php?option=content&task=view&id=3132&Itemid=247.

44. *The New Schaff-Herzog Encyclopedia of Religious Knowledge*, pp. 440-44, 449-50.

45. *The Encyclopedia of Religion*, vol 2, pp. 59-61.

46. *The Jewish Encyclopedia*, vol. II, pp, 499-450.

47. Ron Moseley, "History of the Jewish Mikveh," Arkansas Institute of Holy Land Studies, rmoseley@cei.net.

48. Erich Neumann, *The Great Mother – An Analysis of the Archetype*, p. 59.

49. Ibid, p. 55.

50. *The Gospel of Thomas*, saying 3.

51. Eric Butterworth, *Discover the Power Within*, p. 71.

52. Llewellyn Vaughan-Lee, "Inner Work," You Tube, March 23, 2007.

53. Ellens and Rollins, *Psychology and the Bible, p. 113*.

54. Jamal Rahman, *Sacred Laughter of the Sufis*, p. 10.

55. Thich Nhat Hanh, *Creating True Peace*, pg. 32

56. Charles Fillmore, *Teach Us To Pray*, p. 3.

57. Joel Goldsmith, *The Altitude of Prayer*, p. 26.

58. John A. Sanford, *The Kingdom Within – The Inner Meaning of Jesus' Sayings*, p. 28.

59. Lynn McTaggart, *The Bond – Connecting Through the Space Between Us*, p. 104.

60. *The Way of the Bodhisattva: A Translation of the Bodhicharyavatara*, p.81.

61. Sayings of Gautama Buddha, *Bodhicitta*. www.greatliberation.org., p.3

62. Helene P. Foley, ed., *Homeric Hymn to Demeter*, line 275.

63. Andrew Harvey, *The Divine Feminine, Exploring the Feminine Face of God Around the World*, p. 20.

64. Sharon Salzberg, *Faith, Trusting Your Own Deepest Experience*, p. 12.

65. Jelahuddin Rumi, Coleman Barks, translator, *Selected Poems*, "Let the lover be disgraceful," p. 46.

66. David P. Silverman, *Ancient Egypt*. Hafiz, Daniel Ladinsky, translator, *The Subject Tonight is Love, 60 Wild and Sweet Poems of Hafiz*, p. 47.

67. Jelahuddin Rumi, Coleman Barks translator, *Rumi: The Book of Love: Poems of Ecstasy and Longing*, p. 86.

68. Jelahuddin Rumi, Coleman Barks, translator, *Illuminated Rumi*, p. 3.

69. Langton Hughes, Selected Poems of Langston Hughes, p. 268.

70. Marshall Rosenberg, Ph.D., *Speak Peace in a World of Conflict*, p. 80.

71. Erich Neumann, *The Great Mother – An Analysis of the Archetype*, p. 158.

72. Geshe Lhundba Sopa, ed. David Pratt. *Steps on the Path to Enlightenment*, p. 95.

73. Ravi Ravindra, Ph.D., *The Gospel of John in the Light of Indian Mysticism*, p. 59.

74. Robert A. Emmons,Ph.D., *Thanks! How Practicing Gratitude Can Make You Happier*, pp. 128, 140 & 145.

75. Ibid, p. 58.

76. Margaret Wheatley, *Finding Our Way- Leadership for an Uncertain Time*, p. 136.

77. John A. Sanford, *Mystical Christianity – A Psychological Commentary on the Gospel of John*, p. 168.

78. Elie Wiesel, *Night*, p. xx.

79. Antoinette May, *Pilate's Wife – A Novel of the Roman Empire*. From an interview with the author. www.pilateswife.com/interview.

80. Pema Chodron, *When Things Fall Apart*, p. 12.

81. Eckhart Tolle, *A New Earth*, p. 2.

82. Lao Tze, *Tao Te Ching*, #22.

83. Brown, Brene. TED Talk, http://www.youtube.com/watch?v=X4Qm9cGRub0.

84. Vesela Simic, *Shift: At the Frontiers of Consciousness*, "The Challenge of Forgiveness," Dec., 2006, p. 29.

85. Eric Butterworth, *Discover the Power Within*, p. 15.

86. Cynthia Bouregeault, *The Meaning of Mary Magdalene – Discovering the Woman at the Heart of Christianity*, p. 12.

87. Andrew Harvey, "Blaze of Light, Blood of Creation," *The Unknown She – Eight Faces of an Emerging Consciousness*, p. 105.

88. Jelahuddin Rumi, Coleman Barks, translator, "Guest House," *Essential Rumi*, p. 109.

89. Joan Chamberlain Engelsman, from "The Feminine Dimension of the Divine," *Embracing the Feminine Nature of the Divine*, Tony Boehm, p. 65.

90. Cynthia Avens and Richard Zelley, *Walking the Path of ChristoSophia – Exploring the Hidden Tradition in Christian Spirituality*, p. 30.

91. Gale Berkowitz, "UCLA Study on Friendship Among Women," March 2, 2010, http://www.wellsphere.com.